STOPPING
WORDS
THAT
HURT

STOPPING
WORDS
THAT
HURT

POSITIVE WORDS IN A WORLD
GONE NEGATIVE

DR. MICHAEL D. SEDLER

Chosen
a division of Baker Publishing Group
Minneapolis, Minnesota

© 2001, 2013 by Michael D. Sedler

Revised Edition of *Stop the Runaway Conversation*, 2001.

Originally published as *Stairway to Deception*, Christian Life Publications, 1999.

Published by Chosen Books
11400 Hampshire Avenue South
Bloomington, Minnesota 55438
www.chosenbooks.com

Chosen Books is a division of
Baker Publishing Group, Grand Rapids, Michigan

Printed in the United States of America

Library of Congress Cataloging-in-Publication Data is on file at the Library of Congress, Washington, DC.

ISBN 978-0-8007-9547-4

Cover design by Gearbox

13 14 15 16 17 18 19   7 6 5 4 3 2 1

In Appreciation For . . .

All those who have spoken into my life and helped me become more positive and encouraging in my words and actions.

Baker Publishing Group and the assistance in publishing my books. A special thank-you to Jane Campbell, Natasha Sperling and Karen Steele.

My family: Jason/Rachel/Ella/Charlotte, Aaron, Luke, and my precious wife, Joyce. How blessed I am in life.

Contents

Introduction

In my years as a Christian, I have heard many teachings and presentations on the dangers of gossip, slander and murmuring. Most of these teachings have focused on restraining ourselves from speaking negatively about other people. While I would like to suggest that my desire, like that of most of the people in life, was to bridle my tongue, for many years I was totally unsuccessful in this arena. Time and time again I would find myself speaking negative of others and being involved in critical conversations. This was not only confusing but also frustrating.

In addition, when I was successful at keeping my tongue in check, my ears were being assaulted. I found my thoughts being affected constantly by what others were saying, and they frequently led me down a path of negative impressions toward other people.

Some years ago, while traveling on vacation, my family stopped by a church in southeast Idaho. A visiting minister began to share about the impact of gossip and criticism. Rather than focus on the harm done by speaking negative words, however, he taught about the damage done simply by listening to them. (I later found out this material was from Bill Gothard's "Seminar in Basic Youth Conflicts.") The spirit of conviction fell upon me, and I began a long process of synthesizing the information in order to understand its full implications for my life. As truth was slowly revealed to me in this area, I realized I had been missing an important component of my struggle. Yes, it is true that many of my thoughts and ideas are a problem; the tongue must be controlled; I should not speak evil or negatively of others. However, this constant battle was only a symptom of a much greater problem.

God began to reveal ways in which I fell prey to deception in the area of conversation simply by listening. Many times, for instance, I did not speak a word, yet my very presence "screamed" support for the negative conversation at hand. These "innocent" situations seemed to be more the rule than the exception. This was very disconcerting, as I truly was asking for Christ's character within my life. After many hours, days and months of my seeking God for understanding, He slowly showed specific reasons for my constant stumbling. Whether it was during my times as an educator, counselor, pastor, husband or father, I began to see the traps I had fallen into with my speech patterns. In looking back over the years, I realize that the slowness of His presentation had nothing to do with God and everything to do with my shortsightedness and my inability to grasp the enormity of the problem.

It is the purpose of this book to define and emphasize the magnitude of injury that takes place when we are involved in negative conversations. The Bible refers to negative comments or stories regarding other people as "evil reports." This may seem like a strong term, but a careful search through the Scriptures shows that our gossip and truth-stretching is much more than idle chatter. This type of speech carries with it far-reaching ramifications that affect not only the life of the speaker but the life of the listener. Relationally, this is a life-and-death issue. It is not only "speaking evil" that fosters sin in our lives; *listening to evil reports* defiles our spirits and creates a wedge between friends, family and colleagues.

The Spirit of God desires to touch us, to show us areas where we may have been defiled by evil reports. I believe we can all break away from the enslavement of ungodly habits and *not give ear* to sinful speech patterns. "An evildoer gives heed to false lips; a liar listens eagerly to a spiteful tongue" (Proverbs 17:4). We can become free from listening to negative conversations, and our own tongues will be restrained from speaking evil of others.

This book is about healing, freedom, caring, compassion and love. If we can gain greater control over our own tongues and conversations while limiting the critical comments that we hear in life, we will become a strong encouragement and testimony of God's power in the life of a person.

I encourage you to open your mind, heart and spirit to investigate the part you may play in perpetuating evil or false reports. Be prepared to be challenged, even provoked by this book. The topic is not comfortable, nor are the repercussions of listening to an evil report. Let the Holy Spirit shine light upon each dark, hidden recess of your soul. I pray that God's powerful and gentle hands rest upon each reader to bring purification, illumination and revelation.

I wish to give special thanks and blessings to Mr. Bill Gothard for his inspiration in this area. Also, his willingness to allow me to use some of his material enabled me to build a strong foundation for this book.

1

The Power of the Spoken Word

The world tells us that it is okay to speak negatively about one another. Newspapers, television, magazines and the media in general make millions of dollars exploiting individuals by "sharing" their misfortunes. Talk shows never tire of exposing people in order to create a scandalous atmosphere. Reality shows are based upon embarrassing people and revealing negative areas of a life. Emails, texts, Twitter, Facebook, chat rooms and other social media outlets allow for a fast delivery system of information, regardless of the consequences of the words. We are so brainwashed into believing that it is permissible to violate one another verbally that it takes a concentrated effort to begin to have new thought patterns. Our words may create injury and pain in a life, yet we seem oblivious to the results. As the pages of this book unfold, take time to pray, discuss the topic with others and begin to have your life transformed by the renewing of your mind (see Romans 12:2). Here are a few of the questions that we will address:

- What is meant by an "evil or negative report" and how do I recognize it?
- Is it ever possible to talk about someone without indulging in a negative report?
- Is it still an evil report if those who are speaking do not mean to injure another person?
- What if the report is factual? Is it still considered an "evil report"?
- What if I just listen without comment? Is that not okay?
- I never intend to get involved in negativity, but sometimes the conversation gets away from me. Can I learn to respond in a biblical way to people who gossip and murmur?
- How can I be emotionally, mentally and spiritually cleansed from the violation that occurs when I listen to these reports?

All of these questions ultimately have to do with gaining control of ungodly conversations—those that seem to hook us in and then run out of our control. While portions of this book will deal with the problem of initiating negative comments about others, the greater focus will be on a less understood topic: what to do when others want us to engage in negative conversation with them. We will learn ways to recognize individuals who carry an attitude of negativism and gossip, firm responses to those who attempt to violate others with their speech and positive and effective strategies to prevent us from becoming "evil reporters." The goal: to bring compassion and love to others in a way that will assist them in developing positive speech patterns.

The topic of evil reports is not one that people can ever take lightly. It is not solely a "Christian" issue; it is a life issue for everyone, regardless of personal faith or convictions. As we will see in the chapters that follow, the runaway conversation may begin at a manageable pace. Unless action is taken early on, however, the gossip and murmuring will increase progressively in speed and in the potential for damage. Like a powerful locomotive, the evil report will take us down well-worn tracks of personal defilement and toward a terrible destination: the blindness of deception.

Too strong? We will discuss how easy it is to justify our own behavior even though it may create pain and suffering for others. Evil reports have enormous impact on not only personal relationships but also an individual's spiritual walk with God. Let's begin by understanding just what is meant by an evil report.

NOTE: Though the terms *evil reporter* or *defilement* are used frequently in this chapter (and book), remember they are biblical phrases and should not be seen as judgmental or critical of people. They are identifying characteristics in our lives—areas that need to be weeded out. It is not an indictment on a person nor an attempt to label a person as "evil." We have all fallen prey to these areas and should be excited to be able to have the knowledge base to avoid further pitfalls and traps.

The Evil or False Report

The first word that might come to mind when we consider evil reports is a familiar one: *gossip*. Actually, this is only a small part of what the Bible refers to as an evil or false report. Noah Webster's Dictionary (1828 edition) states that the word *evil* means "having bad qualities of a moral kind; wicked; corrupt;

perverse; producing sorrow, distress, injury or calamity." Thus, an evil report is not only *what* is said but *how* it is said. It involves our attitudes and even the condition of our hearts.

Let's give further substance to the term *evil report*. Here is one working definition that we will use:

> **Evil report:** When an individual maliciously injures, damages or discredits another's reputation or character through the use of words or attitude.

If the intent is to hurt another person's reputation, we must examine our motives.

Ungodly, damaging conversations. How often our words ramble casually and carelessly without any thought as to the repercussions in another person's life! Common comments such as "Did you hear what Tom said to me?" or "I am really offended by Sally. Do you know what she did?" may seem innocuous at first. But if unchecked, this type of speech pattern leads to negative and critical comments about the people involved. It may degrade an individual, eventually creating an atmosphere that provokes others toward feeling wronged and upset and toward eventual separation. We might laugh about nominating certain individuals for the "Ministry of Hurts," but the fallout from this person's conversations leaves a pattern of pain and relationship separation.

Like most of you, I have been on every side of this issue—making the accusations, hearing the accusations and being the brunt of the accusations. In so many of these situations, people (including myself) were misunderstood and injured and suffered emotionally. How can I be a light to the world when I am speaking and listening to darkness? When I was a teacher, I wanted my students and colleagues to feel the support of my words, not the sting of my words. As a parent, I want my children to feel encouraged by my comments, not given license to have negative thoughts and make critical comments about others.

Our careless ways of speaking cannot always be chalked up to "I didn't know better" or "I was only kidding." My desire is to walk a path of integrity, purity and commitment in all my relationships and interactions. In fact, I believe that when we fall into the pattern of gossip, criticism and negative reports, we are making a major faux pas in life. Proverbs 10:18 says that "whoever spreads slander is a fool."

I know of a young couple who are considering marriage. This is an exciting topic among their social circle. Once when asked about the possibility of getting engaged, the young man responded, "Slowly and surely, we'll be engaged." One friend in the group, who had overheard part of the conversation, turned toward another friend and said, "Who and Shirley are getting engaged? And who's Shirley?" It is so easy to take a comment, twist it and run with it. Our words are like toothpaste coming out of the tube. It flows out so easily yet is impossible to put back into the container. To prevent further loss of toothpaste, we need to take the cap and place it over the tube. And with people, the cap (mouth) needs to be closed with haste, before words flow out too quickly.

Let's take another approach. Imagine filling out a "daily life application." How would you answer the following questions?

1. Do you speak negatively about others?

2. When you are hurt by another person's insensitivity, do you confront him or her directly, or do you share the frustration with others?

3. If Christ was listening to each of your conversations (and He is), would the content be offensive to Him?

4. When you disagree with your supervisor, who else is going to know about it?

If this does not seem challenging enough, change the phrases a bit. Instead of *another person* or *supervisor* try *spouse* or *parent*. Ouch!

There are those (perhaps even reading this book) who feel gossip is a social function, an acceptable part of everyday life. One person attempted to convince me that prior to current communication trends and devices, gossip was a positive way to share about events, neighbors and situations. If this is your belief as well, please continue to read this book. You will clearly see the difference between sharing about events and people in a loving, positive, educational and compassionate way and sharing about others in an effort to cause pain and hurt in their lives.

Tested by Fire

Daniel 3 relates the story of three Hebrew companions who had been brought with Daniel into exile. Their names were Hananiah, Mishael and Azariah. You might recognize their Babylonian names more readily—Shadrach, Meshach and Abednego. This story, as you may recall, tells how King Nebuchadnezzar ordered a golden idol to be erected and commanded that all the people in the province fall down and worship it. He declared that all who refused to fall down would be cast into a fiery furnace, thereby being consumed by heat and flames. The three Hebrew men, however, refused to disobey God by worshiping an idol.

Because these men refused to bow down before the false god, murmuring arose among some of the people. It was not long before the king heard about Shadrach, Meshach and Abednego. Though this is a familiar Bible story, many of you may not have realized that the king came to the knowledge of the three Hebrew men via gossip and criticism.

Think about it. In the entire kingdom of Babylon, how would he notice three people not bowing down? It was brought to his attention by the Chaldeans. They were the "wise people of the land." You can read more about them in Daniel 1:4, 2:2 and chapters 4 and 5. The Chaldeans interpreted dreams, and their language and literature were used in the land. How do you think they felt when they were displaced by foreigners, strangers, Hebrews? Exactly—they were upset and jealous. Therefore, an evil report was used to damage, cause injury and exact vengeance against the reputation of these people.

Sidenote: Though the report was accurate and true, it was still a negative or evil report due to the intended purpose of the report—to bring about the destruction of Shadrach, Meshach and Abednego.

When told of these men not bowing down to the idol, the king was very angry. He had the three men brought before him, confirmed their refusal to bow down to the idol and commanded that they be thrown into a furnace of fire. Then the soldiers and king looked on, anticipating the young men's incineration. Instead, before their eyes, a fourth figure appeared within the furnace.

> Then King Nebuchadnezzar was astonished; and he rose in haste and spoke, saying to his counselors, "Did we not cast three men bound into the midst of the fire?" They answered and said to the king, "True, O king." "Look!" he answered, "I see four men loose, walking in the midst of the fire; and they are not hurt, and the form of the fourth is like the Son of God."
>
> Daniel 3:24–25

Astonished and somewhat in fear, the king released Shadrach, Meshach and Abednego and immediately promoted them to positions of honor within the province. The king then expressed honor toward the God who had so miraculously saved His people and declared further that no one would speak "anything amiss" against this God.

This is an inspiring and exciting account about people of faith. Those who honored God were blessed and found favor in His sight. Well, perhaps not everyone. What of Nebuchadnezzar? Was he defiled and contaminated by taking part in an evil report? Were there repercussions for his acting on ungodly words and not repenting? What can happen to those who do not have a godly response to evil reports?

By listening to an evil report, King Nebuchadnezzar was polluted. His perspective of the situation was skewed. Without seeking further information, he chose to take the lives of three people because of a negative report, and even though he later acknowledged the reality of one true God, he did not repent of his actions and learn humility. In Daniel 4 we find the rest of the story regarding the king. And make note: The king did not *initiate* an evil report against the Hebrew men, but he *listened* to one and, thereby, became defiled by it. We read here that the king rose up in pride and arrogance. He proclaimed *his* accomplishments and *his* achievements.

> At the end of the twelve months [Nebuchadnezzar] was walking about the royal palace of Babylon. The king spoke, saying, "Is not this great Babylon, that *I* have built for a royal dwelling by *my* mighty power and for the honor of *my* majesty?" While the word was still in the king's mouth, a voice fell from heaven: "King Nebuchadnezzar, to you it is spoken: the kingdom has departed from you!"
>
> Daniel 4:29–31, emphasis added

Defilement will often take the form of pride and selfishness. Due to his self-centered approach, King Nebuchadnezzar's kingdom was taken from him. He was humiliated and lived for a time in the fields, eating grass like an animal. This came about due to his own words found in Daniel 3:28–29, where he condemns anyone who speaks against the God of Shadrach, Meshach and Abednego.

In time, however, he did repent, turned his heart toward God and was restored. This was only done, however, through humility and recognition of his own arrogance and pride.

> At the same time my reason returned to me, and for the glory of my kingdom, my honor and splendor returned to me. My counselors and nobles resorted to me, I was restored to my kingdom, and excellent majesty was added to me. Now I, Nebuchadnezzar, praise and extol and honor the King of heaven, all of whose works are truth, and His ways justice. And those who walk in pride He is able to put down.
>
> Daniel 4:36–37

It is imperative that you understand this truth: *Just listening* to an evil report can do tremendous damage to your perspective, viewpoint and overall spirit. Nebuchadnezzar should not have allowed himself to be part of the plot to destroy the Hebrew people. His refusal to ask questions, gain clarification and remove himself from the plan of destruction led to an impurity in his own spirit.

Stop a moment and think about your own experiences. Have you ever heard negative comments about a person and then let it impact your own perspective?

This is a serious issue in our lives and for those around us. Joining in a negatively driven conversation, no matter how small the participation, may destroy the testimony of a life. Listening to grumbling and ungodly attitudes eventually contaminates the spirit. The more we allow discontent to be taken in by our spirits, the greater the tendency to compromise our own speech patterns. We are being called to a high standard of living where the rewards for our faithfulness are eternal.

EXAMINING THE HEART

1. In your own life, have you developed speech patterns that would be considered evil reports (as defined in this chapter)?

2. When you were growing up, were gossip, rumors and false reporting encouraged, modeled or demonstrated by the adults in the home?

3. Think back over the years and try to remember if the topic of this book has been taught in your church. Your home? Your school?

2

Here Comes the Pitch:
Being on the Alert

As a youth in Phoenix, Arizona, I played baseball during my elementary and high school years. I was the fortunate recipient of a scholarship and played baseball at a university in San Diego, California. I learned a lot from my high school and college coaches about preparing for the team and the pitcher we would be facing in each game. After graduating I spent many years coaching Little Leaguers, high school teams and summer league elite teams.

This experience taught me that it is possible during a game to determine the type of pitch that is coming at the batter. At the Little League level this is easy. Each pitch is a soft lob that, if the prevailing winds are favorable, might make it to the plate. As the players progress in skills, however, the batter can face a variety of pitches ranging from a fastball to a change-up to a slider to a curve. And each of those pitches might have several variations. It is always of great advantage to the hitters to know what type of pitch is coming to the plate, particularly in the professional leagues when the ball can fly toward a batter at upwards of 95 miles an hour.

Telegraphing the Pitch

One aspect my coaches taught me was to discover flaws in the pitcher's delivery. Did the pitcher kick his leg higher to throw a fastball? Was his glove more open when he pitched a curveball? Was his arm lower when he threw a slider? This is called "telegraphing the pitch." It allows the batter to anticipate more accurately what type of pitch is coming. With the guesswork out of the way, the batter can concentrate on one thing: hitting the ball.

The process is not unlike an experience with someone who tosses an evil report our way. Unfortunately, people who violate others with their words (remember, these people are often *us*) do not carry signs saying, "Here comes an evil report high and on the inside!" It would be fantastic if we had such obvious warnings in order to prepare for negative attitudes and words. As with many successful pitchers, these people "mix up" or vary their approaches, making it difficult to ascertain what is coming. The result is often confusion for the recipient of the negative report and unwitting involvement in what soon becomes a runaway conversation.

The good news, however, is that those who tend toward gossip and spreading rumors often "telegraph" their pitches. That is, I believe that they give some key indicators that let us know what pitch is coming. This chapter will examine those methods of delivering an evil report. Being aware can help prevent our being duped or taken in by a seemingly sincere desire to "get guidance" or "just talk" or "share what's on my heart" when the true intention is gossip. Note also that, in this particular case, the posture of "Don't blame me, I'm just the messenger" does not apply, because it is the messenger (as well as the message) that may be on the brink of violating the listener's spirit.

How do we identify the message of one who is sending de-filing attitudes and conversations our way? Listed below are eight tactics (or strategies) used by those who are messengers of defiling information. Knowing these ploys will help us to ferret out the true motives of the speaker and thereby protect our spirits from violation and defilement. Unfortunately, I came across these methods through my own trial and (definitely) error over the years.

I want to emphasize again that people who are conduits of critical conversations are not necessarily mean or evil people. Like us, they may be hurt emotionally and sharing from a wounded perspective. They may be angry or upset, looking for a little revenge. We are not evaluating the following conversation styles in an effort to categorize or judge another person. Our goal is to identify potential approaches in order to bring guidance and support toward a gentler conversation.

Identifying the Actions of Evil Reporters

Looks for support from you for his beliefs, attitudes or actions

Do you find yourself regarding the situation with a sympathetic ear? Do you feel the need to be helpful? And what signals do you give in response? Do you raise your eyebrows in interest? Do you lean in closer, suggesting, "I want to hear this"? Do you actually say, "Tell me more"?

The Bible tells a story, found in the book of Esther, about a man named Haman who gave an evil report and found a sympathetic ear. Haman, an officer in the court of King Ahasuerus, held the highest seat among all of the princes. Further, the king had commanded that all of the people in his realm pay homage to Haman. As with our story earlier from the book of Daniel, here, too, a faithful Hebrew man refused to bow down to anyone but God. This Jewish man was named Mordecai, and he was Queen Esther's cousin and guardian, although her lineage was unknown to the king.

When Haman learned that Mordecai refused to bow down and acknowledge his authority, he was furious. But rather than lay hands on Mordecai alone, Haman decided to do away with all the Jews throughout the whole kingdom. Angered and full of jealousy, Haman approached the king.

> Then Haman said to King Ahasuerus, "There is a certain people scattered and dispersed among the people in all the provinces of your kingdom; their laws are different from all other people's, and they do not keep the king's laws. Therefore it is not fitting for the king to let them remain. If it pleases the king, let a decree be written that they be destroyed, and I will pay ten thousand talents of silver into the hands of those who do the work, to bring it into the king's treasuries."
>
> Esther 3:8–9

The king's response was to give his signet ring to Haman in order to validate the decree. Haman must have tested the king's spirit many times, for he knew the king would respond in pride and jealousy. There is no indication of the king's questioning Haman's report; his response is one of total acceptance. While Haman used the phrase "if it pleases the king," he "tipped off his pitch" with two key sentences. First, he told (not asked) the king what was "fitting for the king" to allow, and then he offered to pay money out of his own pocket for the destruction of the people. His obvious self-interest in the issue should have been enough for the king to ask a few questions, such as "Is their destruction that important to you that you would pay from your own hands?" or "I have never noticed this before; how is it that it bothers you so much?" The king was so interested in supporting Haman and acknowledging the authority that he had placed upon him that he did not question Haman's actions.

It is usual for most of us to listen without questioning. We oftentimes want to support a friend, supervisor or person of influence. In fact, a messenger may single us out because she knows we will not disagree with or question her. Are we being used because of our own gullibility and blindness to negative speech patterns?

Tries to distract you from a God-given focus or course of action

In Nehemiah 6 this method was used in an attempt to dissuade Nehemiah from rebuilding the walls of Jerusalem. Four times his enemies sent someone to distract him; four times he refused to leave the work on the wall (see verse 4). A fifth distraction was a letter alleging that the Jewish people and Nehemiah were planning a rebellion and that he intended to be crowned their king. But Nehemiah did not take the bait. He refused to leave his work.

The story of Nehemiah emphasizes that carriers of negative conversations do not stop after one attempt. If one pitch does not work, then look out! Here comes another one! In verse 10 we find Nehemiah being approached for the sixth time.

[Shemaiah] said, "Let us meet together in the house of God, within the temple, and let us close the doors of the temple, for they are coming to kill you; indeed, at night they will come to kill you."

Here was an even stronger report intending to garner an emotional response from Nehemiah and cause him to sin by entering and hiding in the Temple. Would he take part in the conversation? Would he allow his emotions to carry him away? No, he was unflappable. Verse 11 records his response: "I said, 'Should such a man as I flee? And who is there such as I who would go into the temple to save his life? I will not go in!'" It was Nehemiah's refusal to engage in the conversation that allowed him to receive insight from God.

> Then I perceived that God had not sent him at all. . . . For this reason he was hired, that I should be afraid and act that way and sin, so that they might have cause for an evil report, that they might reproach me.
>
> verses 12–13

Nehemiah recognized the indicators given by the transgressors and was able to avoid the entanglement of the enemy.

Once again we see an interesting aspect of a negative report. Verse 10 clearly promotes the idea of Nehemiah going into the Temple to hide. And if he had entered the Temple, it would have been considered a sin. After all, in those days, not everybody could enter the Temple. And in verse 11, Nehemiah states that Shemaiah was pressing him toward being afraid and sinning (going into the Temple) and that it would be cause for an evil report against Nehemiah.

Here are some questions to consider and a potential epiphany for some.

- If Nehemiah had entered the Temple, would it have been a sin? (I believe the answer is yes.)

- Would Shemaiah have used this to give an evil report? (Again, yes.)
- But would it not have been a true story being shared by Shemaiah? (Absolutely.)

So we can assume that because something is true (going into the Temple) and it is reported by another person, it still might be an "evil report." Why? Because, as Nehemiah states, they were using it so "they might reproach me." The report or conversation was not for encouragement, restoration or support. It was to injure Nehemiah. Again, we see that a true statement or conversation about someone might be considered a negative report based on the purpose of the conversation.

Attempts to create disunity and division

The Pharisees commonly used this pitch by trying to separate the people from Jesus. They wanted to suggest to His followers and their own leaders that Jesus was blasphemous, sacrilegious or a violator of the Word of God.

> And the chief priests and the scribes . . . watched Him, and sent spies who pretended to be righteous, that they might seize on His words, in order to deliver Him to the power and the authority of the governor.
>
> Luke 20:19–20

Remember some of the ongoing comments from the Pharisees: "Should we pay taxes to Caesar?" "Why do you heal on the Sabbath?" "Why do you associate with sinners?" All good questions, but the purpose and attitude were to separate and create disunity among the people.

We might well believe that phrases like "Wait until I tell you about the adulterous woman!" and "Have you heard the blasphemy he uttered?" were being spewed forth from their lips daily. Any listeners who were not on guard could have been led by curiosity into disunity.

Shows anger when you disagree with her

One way to determine the motives of the individual who is sharing a report is to watch her reactions when you disagree with her. Anger and defensiveness are obvious signs that the person has a strong personal motive. She has an emotional investment and wants to gain support for her side of the story.

Imagine the response from Judas when Jesus did not support his desire to hoard precious oil and allowed it to be used to anoint His feet:

> Then Mary took a pound of very costly oil of spikenard, anointed the feet of Jesus, and wiped His feet with her hair. And the house was filled with the fragrance of the oil. But one of His disciples, Judas Iscariot, Simon's son, who would betray Him, said, "Why was this fragrant oil not sold for three hundred denarii and given to the poor?" This he said, not that he cared for the poor, but because he was a thief, and had the money box; and he used to take what was put in it. But Jesus said, "Let her alone; she has kept this for the day of My burial. For the poor you have with you always, but Me you do not have always."
>
> John 12:3–8

Ironically, it is in the next chapter of John that Jesus identifies His betrayer. No doubt Judas was angry at being rebuffed by Jesus. He allowed unforgiveness to burn in his heart and it destroyed him.

I have heard it said that "Unforgiveness is like taking a poison but expecting the other person to die." How often have we swallowed the pill of unforgiveness and then used negative and critical statements to get back at someone? In the end, it only hurts us and turns us into bitter people.

Approaches with an apparent humble and modest attitude

By appearing to need your advice and guidance, she might portray herself as unable to figure something out. This is very common for the experienced carrier of an evil report. "Could I ask your opinion on something?" While this sounds innocent, your nod of approval will generally bring an onslaught of gossip: "Yesterday Jenny did something really awful. She went to this movie and . . ."

If you do not stop the forward progression of gossip right away, your curiosity will be aroused, and before you know it, you will have listened to an evil report about Jenny. This messenger did not really want any advice or guidance. If you were to ask her why she told you about the incident, more than likely she would reply that she was not sure if she should do something about it or tell someone about it. In other words, she decided to use any listeners she could find as testing ground. Defilement comes in subtle and quick ways.

Here are a few simple questions that might be used to draw you into a conversation by tapping in to your curiosity. Oftentimes, our experiences with a person have allowed us to identify him as a potential gossip. The quick responses can help turn the gossip aside.

Question: "Can you keep a secret?" Response: "Not really."

Question: "Did you hear about Carol?" Response: "Yes, isn't she a sweet person?"

Question: "Wait until you hear about Tim." Response: "Okay, I'll wait. I am sort of busy now. Thanks."

Okay, maybe some of these ideas are a bit tongue-in-cheek. However, we need to find strategies to minimize the runaway conversations. Our response should not be sarcastic or critical, but one of kindness and sensitivity. We are attempting to help the person from being a deliverer of negative information. And this will reduce the tendency for us to listen to critical speech.

Attempts to show off his power, strength or authority

Due to the nature of their jobs, the important people they know or the ability to be in the right place at the right time, some people gain advancement in their jobs or status. Some of these people like to take advantage of this positioning by showing off their newfound authority. They look for continued worldly encouragement based on temporary moments of recognition. Be on the lookout for this type of insecurity in those around you. It is a possible sign that information may be forthcoming that will violate your spirit.

This happens because they use knowledge as a power base to lure others in. Many people respond to the power of knowledge by desiring it. The devil's attempt to cause Jesus to sin, found in Matthew 4, is a classic example of this type of approach.

> Again, the devil took Him up on an exceedingly high mountain, and showed Him all the kingdoms of the world and their glory. And he said to Him, "All these things I will give You if You will fall down and worship me."
>
> Matthew 4:8–9

The carrier of an evil report uses his position of knowledge to attract us and place us in a position to stumble. There is certainly nothing wrong with being wealthy or being in a strong

32

position of authority. We just need to be sure we wield this power in love and use it as an instrument of encouragement and support for others.

Flatters and praises you

Think back to the last time someone spoke flattering words to you. (If you cannot remember, that may be a good sign.) It is common for people who want something or desire to influence your thinking to use compliments as a way to set up their approach. You have probably heard a youngster say, "You are the best mom in the world," quickly followed by, "Can I have some money to go to the store?"

This is not to suggest that every compliment is intended to manipulate your emotions. There should be many times when sincere words of praise are offered simply for encouragement. I desire to compliment and praise my wife and children as a source of strength and love. However, we need to be aware that flattery is also a tool one may use when attempting to manipulate and deposit an evil report within another person. The praise or flattery prepares a listener to receive the report by creating a more receptive spirit.

The armed forces employ the strategy of using military power (troops, artillery, bombs) to wear down the enemy prior to a big strike. This is referred to as "softening the enemy." Likewise, people will use words to "soften" us before they come at us with a larger attack. They prey upon our pride, insecurity and desire for recognition. After all, if a person thinks I have great ideas and is simply asking for my perspective, why shouldn't I listen and then give feedback? The answer is that I should not listen because I will become polluted and my perceptions will become distorted. "Therefore do not associate with one who flatters with his lips" (Proverbs 20:19).

Unfortunately, there is something in us that desires attention and recognition. We may yearn for acceptance and a need for someone to listen to us and our perspective. The mere opportunity to share "what I think" is often too much to pass up. This person will draw from this area of a life and anticipate that we will be sucked into the whirlpool of gossip.

Naturally, there are appropriate times to share and give feedback to others. Our personal perspective may help bring understanding to a difficult situation. We need to carefully evaluate situations to prevent being hooked by the bait of gossip.

Embellishes and exaggerates a situation to make it seem worse than it really is

In Numbers 13 we read that God spoke to Moses regarding the land of Canaan: "And the LORD spoke to Moses, saying, 'Send men to spy out the land of Canaan, *which I am giving to the children of Israel*'" (verses 1–2, emphasis added). Notice it was not a question of whether or not they should invade the land of Canaan. God had already stated that He was giving it to them.

However, ten of those spies came back with an evil report. They became detectives of darkness, exaggerating and evoking wild imaginations among the people.

> And they gave the children of Israel a bad report of the land which they had spied out, saying, "The land through which we have gone as spies is a land that devours its inhabitants, and all the people whom we saw in it are men of great stature. There we saw the giants . . . and we were like grasshoppers in our own sight, and so we were in their sight."
>
> Numbers 13:32–33

The people of Israel listened, became frightened and departed from their faith in God. This is exactly what happens when we

34

listen to evil reports. Our carnal minds take over and overwhelm our spirits of faith. Suddenly, what was possible through God is now impossible even to imagine. The larger the problem, the more overwhelmed we become at attempting to solve it.

Each one of these eight areas creates an atmosphere of confusion, critical perspectives and fear. And the fact is, the world is full of these types of discussions. But because we now know to anticipate the possibility of negative conversations, we can guard our spirits and be on the lookout for times when we might be susceptible. Proverbs 11:9 says, "Dishonest people use gossip to destroy their neighbors; good people are protected by their own good sense" (CEV). We all need to pray and ask for God's wisdom so that we can be protected with good sense.

The pitcher eyes home plate; he winds up; here comes the pitch. . . .

Remember, if we are on the alert, we can foresee the pitch coming toward us. We can choose not to receive it. We can be prepared for the traps of the enemy. Be sensitive, be kind, show compassion and love, but stand firm in your convictions. Greater damage will occur by falling into the traps of listening to negative conversations than showing wisdom and refusing to be a part of gossip and criticism.

===== EXAMINING THE HEART =====

1. Are you able to think of one person whom you would identify as a carrier of evil reports?

2. What is the impact on you when this person begins to share negative reports?

3. How might you respond differently?

3

Controlling the Tongue

Many of us may now begin to see multiple times that we have been lured into runaway conversations by listening to the opening remarks of an evil report. We may be surprised to find ourselves involved before we even realize what has happened to us. It is important not to be too harsh on ourselves (or the other person) when this happens. As we begin to identify old patterns and develop new listening skills, we will become more and more adept at not taking part in this repetitive behavior. But our focus must change. We must have our antennas up and be prepared when we hear negative comments and subtle innuendos about others. This is especially true when we find ourselves with certain people or in specific situations that in the past have been filled with defiling conversations. Remember the old adage "Fool me once, shame on you; fool me twice, shame on me."

I was recently at a family gathering when, as had happened in the past, the conversation began to turn to negative talk and gossip. I made a comment regarding the negative nature of the conversation and that the person was not present to defend (or clarify) the situation. This did not dissuade anyone; the conversation continued. Again I spoke up about not making negative comments about others. While I was not about to win any popularity contests at that moment, I did finally get my point across. For the next few days when a conversation would lean toward gossip, they would look at me and make a comment like, "We better not say anything bad or Mike will tell us to stop." I did not mind this at all. In fact, it only encouraged me to draw the line a little sooner in future conversations.

Remember, people do not usually get caught up in sin without prior warning. Adultery, stealing, lying, cheating and other areas of sin often occur by a slow seduction of our flesh and minds. If we allow these strongholds to permeate our thoughts and emotions, we will be deceived. If we get on the train, we will go where it takes us. Once we are aware of the patterns of our life and those of the world, we can begin to be proactive and prevent falling into temptation.

I read a little story that talks about the patterns and habits of life. It reminds me of the traps we fall into regarding negative reports.

"An Autobiography in Five Short Chapters"

Chapter 1: "I walk down the street. There is a deep hole in the sidewalk and I fall in. I am lost. . . . I am helpless. It isn't my fault. It takes forever to find a way out."

Chapter 2: "I walk down the same street. There is a deep hole in the sidewalk. I pretend I don't see it. I fall in, again. I can't believe I am in this same place. But it isn't my fault. It still takes a long time to get out."

Chapter 3: "I walk down the same street. There is a deep hole in the sidewalk. I see it is there. I still fall in. . . . It is a habit. . . . But my eyes are open. I know where I am. It is my fault. I get out immediately."

Chapter 4: "I walk down the same street. There is a deep hole in the sidewalk. I walk around it."

Chapter 5: "I walk down another street."

Author Unknown

This story illustrates the tendency to develop a repetitive cycle of sin via well-worn patterns. You and I can begin to overcome these habits and prevent them from occurring by our willingness to learn new patterns. The opening chapters of this book allowed me to formalize a definition for an evil report and look at some of its opening pitches. Here is the initial definition:

When an individual maliciously injures, damages or discredits another's reputation or character through the use of words or attitude.

And here is an expansion of that definition:

An unauthorized, distorted or false report that influences us to form a negative (or evil) opinion about another person.

The ensuing pages of this chapter explore different ways to examine someone's motives and intentions *before* listening to or being influenced by his or her full report. We can begin to train our minds and our response patterns to discourage certain types of conversations, narrowing the chances of hearing a false report. We do this by directing questions and statements to the carrier of the evil report, thus demanding clarification and a thoughtful response. Not only will this help you, the listener, but it will allow those speakers who desire to be godly not to violate another person through murmuring. As they check their own spirits, they might recognize the danger of slandering another individual.

Imagine a scene from a typical day. You are sitting at work, home, school or church minding your own business and having no trouble feeling spiritually clean. Suddenly out of the blue Kathy says, "Did you hear about William?" As a natural (and habitual) response, you say, "No, what?" She begins to talk and share a negative report. A red flag is sent up; sirens begin to go off in your mind; a little voice says, "Warning! Warning! Danger ahead!"

What do you say? Can you simply walk away? It is very common for us to feel trapped and, therefore, allow people to continue in these conversations even if we feel defiled and uncomfortable.

My youngest son, Luke, was listening to my wife and me discuss this book. Joyce was asking for clarification in an effort to help focus some of my own thoughts. Luke interrupted us and said, "If someone is telling you something bad about another person, all you need to do is turn to him and say, 'Gossip, gossip, gossip, gossip!'" After my wife and I stopped laughing, I realized that was actually a pretty good strategy. I am sure it would cut off the conversation quickly. But just in case you are not as bold as my son, the following questions and statements are practical and easy to use in the midst of negative conversations.

Questions to Ask

"Is this something you think I need to hear about?"

This question asks the person to substantiate the legitimacy of telling *you*. While it may be important for someone to know the information, are you the one who should be told? He may respond with a hesitant, "Well, I'm not sure." Ask him to think about it further before sharing any more with you. This comment will also help any person who is not intentionally meaning to gossip and is unknowingly about to do so. It makes a break in what could be a growing habit in the person's life.

I was recently in a counseling session with a man who was separated from his wife. We were preparing for a reconciliation meeting. At one point, he said, "You probably don't know this about Karen, but when she was younger—" I interrupted him immediately and said, "Terry, if Karen hasn't told me, then I don't want to hear it from you." He agreed and we went on with the rest of the session. If it had been critical information for reconciliation purposes, Terry could have brought it up with Karen in the room. It is common to find people who know that gossip and murmuring are wrong yet are still parties to both. This is especially true when they are hurt or angry. When confronted, they will admit they do not like it but that it is a bad habit. Your gentle yet firm approach can help break this pattern.

"What specific parts of this conversation need to be discussed with me?"

This type of question is a little more specific and gives the person an opportunity to gain self-control, while you do the same. It compels an individual to choose consciously to tell you information. There are times when a person will take me through a ten-minute scenario before getting to the actual point of the story. In this case, I want just the facts. I want the individual to stick to the main points of the issue and cut out the extraneous parts. The more that the speaker must carefully dissect the story, the more she may cut away negative and biased comments. Shorter is better in many cases. Remember, just by the act of listening we are indirectly supporting and encouraging the speaker to continue to share information.

"I am going to take notes so I can recall details. Do you mind?"

This statement and question may cause some uneasiness in the transmitter of a negative report. People do not like to be held accountable for murmuring and gossiping. It is very common at this point for the person to change his story and his tack with you. It was during one counseling session that an individual began to say negative things about another person in the church. I took out a notepad and said, "Please continue. I just want to be sure I hear you correctly so we can sit down with this sister and work through a reconciliation process."

At this point, the individual stopped and said, "Well, I probably shouldn't say anything else until I talk with her." Amen! There is something about putting words in writing that creates hesitation and even fear in people. (We call it accountability.)

In case you are a little uncomfortable with the idea of taking notes, think about the number of people who take notes during a discussion: doctors, accountants, electricians, counselors, plumbers, to name a few. I frequently encourage educators to take notes when talking with parents. It allows us to accurately remember what is being said while also holding people accountable for their words.

"Who told you this information?"

This is a critical question to ask and should be said softly and without an edge of accusation. Once again you are calling the speaker into accountability. And I can imagine the response: "I am not supposed to tell." When someone refuses to identify the source of the information, it is a sure sign of hiddenness, secrecy and a potentially evil report.

If the person does divulge the source of the information, it is important to probe a little further. "Does Tony know you are telling me this?" "Will Keri feel comfortable knowing you are sharing this with others?" Or even, "Since Debbie was the source of this information, perhaps she should be here when we talk." The key point is that people want to remain as anonymous as possible in most situations. By having them commit to names, we can then begin to get to the root of the motive for the statement. Was it a former friend, one who had a recent argument with the person? Is this an individual who, like Haman, has something to gain from destroying a reputation?

Many times it is almost impossible to track down the original source of false reports. Do you remember the game called "Telephone"? Ten to fifteen people stand in a circle. One person whispers a statement into the ear of the person next to him and then that person quietly whispers the comment to the next person. The phrase or story is passed from person to person. Often a key word or portion of the story is inadvertently left out, mostly due to poor or selective listening. When the last person hears the story and then tells the group what he has heard, it is usually very different from its original form. "Telephone" is humorous because it is a game. In reality, though, distorted facts and story changes in which "truth becomes stranger than fiction" can be deadly. Do not be a part of this cycle. Refuse to be a listener of a negative report.

> *"Is this your opinion/interpretation of something you have heard, or did you actually observe this situation?"*

Remember the second definition of an evil report shared earlier in this chapter: An unauthorized, distorted or false report that influences us to form an evil opinion about another person. It is possible to share facts and yet misrepresent them due to the essence (or nature) of our hearts. We see this in the advertising and marketing business. A portion of the facts (or only favorable facts) is presented to the consumer. This controls the perception of the product in the mind of the public. In the case of an evil report, you are the consumer. The person sharing a report with you may tell you only a portion of the situation. He or she may taint the story with facial expressions, body language and little comments that influence your receptivity to the information.

Let me remind you that while false reports are always evil reports, evil reports are not necessarily false reports. Suppose Sherry tells this information to a friend of hers: "Did you hear about James and Tonya? They got into a really big argument and talked about getting a divorce. And to think he is an elder in the church and she is part of the Sunday school ministry. How can they get a divorce and call themselves Christians?" The truth of the situation may be that James and Tonya had an argument and that the words "Maybe we should have never gotten married" and "We'd be better off divorced" were spoken. What Sherry neglected to mention, however, was that the couple have since talked through this issue and are working on changing their behavior patterns. Having the reporter check out the validity and the facts of the situation will help prevent rumors from spreading.

It is imperative to remember that we are not obligated to listen while another person shares evil reports. Asking questions and clarifying and challenging the speaker's motives may be necessary to protect ourselves from being victims of defilement. If the speaker observed or was a part of the situation, there may well be hurts, confusion and perception problems to be addressed. If the speaker got the information secondhand, we certainly must consider the possibility that facts have been distorted.

In John 18:33–34, Pilate asks Jesus a question. Jesus responds to Pilate using a variation of this approach. Jesus says, "Are you speaking for yourself about this, or did others tell you this concerning Me?" What a great question to ask someone. "Are these your thoughts or did they come from elsewhere?"

"May I quote you when I check this out?"

Those who give an evil report often claim to be misquoted. How many times do we see this in the newspaper? "'The senator is a cheating, lying politician who should never be trusted,' says his political opponent." The next day we read, "The political opponent says he was misquoted and the information was taken out of context." Naturally, the initial report is on the front page while the retraction or clarification is on the fourteenth page! Stating that I was misquoted allows me to avoid admitting that I gave a false report. I neither accept responsibility nor feel the need to ask for forgiveness.

Asking a person if he objects to being quoted is another way to create a sense of accountability. In order to protect himself he might say, "Oh no! Don't quote me. It would hurt her feelings if she knew I told you," or "She would be mad at me." If a person is unwilling to stand up for what he or she has said, something is amiss.

And why would someone be upset for sharing information unless it was of a negative nature? Certainly, if I was telling someone in order to help another person, to bring support to them or even to gain more assistance, most people would not be angry for telling another person.

"Before you share any further, what are you expecting from me?"

This will help clarify the ground rules of the conversation. Through this question, you bring to light the purpose behind sharing the information and the expectation that comes with it. Is it to receive prayer? Is it to get counsel and guidance? Do you need other ideas or feedback? Is it to spread gossip and slander? (Bingo!)

When I was teaching sixth graders, gossip (or tattling) was a common problem. During recess a child would often come to me and complain that someone took her basketball or pushed her down. This had a tendency to result in students being reprimanded. It was on a cold, snowy day that I understood for the first time the manipulation taking place from these chronic tattlers. On this day Carol told me that José threw a snowball in her direction. I was cold and distracted and decided to dismiss it as a minor incident. Carol pressed it, however, asking me, "Aren't you going to do anything?" With understanding beginning to dawn, I responded, "What would you like me to do?" Carol said, "He should be in trouble and miss recess. That's what always happens when I tell the teachers about José."

Carol had her mind made up as to what her expectations were from me. If these expectations were not met, arguing, complaining and whining were sure to follow in an effort to get her way. I spent some time with Carol over the next days trying to help her see the impact of getting others into trouble. I believe this not only helped her to understand the difference between tattling and sharing a serious concern, but helped place boundaries on her further conversations about other people. From then on, prior to giving any answers, I would ask Carol, "What are you expecting from me?" or "What kind of answer will satisfy you?" This approach helps to get covert agendas placed on top of the table where they can be dealt with.

"Do you agree with (or find validity in) this situation as it has been presented to you?"

Another way to say this is, "How do you personally feel about this situation?" I like to personalize the problem and have the individual analyze it biblically. Is the incident consistent with what we know about the people involved? Are we looking for a solution? Ask the person what the Bible says about the issues. How would Jesus handle the problem? What can be done to help those involved? The individual may ask for your impressions of the situation.

This gives you an excellent opportunity to respond with something like this: "It probably is something the people involved need to talk about and decide on a direction" or "It really doesn't matter what I think since it has nothing to do with me" or even "I think we need to pray for them right now. Will you join me?"

"Have you spoken to those people who are directly involved with this situation?"

If the messenger of a report wants to tell you of a dispute between two other people, you can respond with the fact that the Bible is very clear as to the procedure in such a situation. Matthew 18:15 says, "Moreover if your brother sins against you, go and tell him his fault between you and him alone. If he hears you, you have gained your brother."

We will talk about this in more depth in a later chapter. This offers a wonderful opportunity to share the importance of approaching one another in love in an effort to restore our brothers and sisters. While some of us want to believe we have a "gift of exposing," we *should seek* the "ministry of restoration." Spirituality is not measured by how well we expose an offender but by how effectively we assist in the effort to restore an offender.

> Brethren, if a man is overtaken [or caught] in any trespass, you who are spiritual restore such a one in a spirit of gentleness, considering yourself lest you also be tempted. Bear one another's burdens, and so fulfill the law of Christ.
>
> Galatians 6:1–2

I like the way this Scripture is written in the Contemporary English Version:

> My friends, you are spiritual. So if someone is trapped in sin, you should gently lead that person back to the right path. But watch out, and don't be tempted yourself. You obey the law of Christ when you offer each other a helping hand.

"It is important for me to pray about this (or think about it, get counsel from others, etc.) before I respond to you."

This is an excellent way to model the fact that you are not about to make a quick decision or respond emotionally. Quite often the situation being discussed will affect you personally. This is why the person has chosen to tell you. By guarding your emotions and your personal response, however, you will prevent yourself from becoming a part of the cycle of gossip.

The above questions and statements will help us gain a better understanding of the motivation of the reporter. *There are legitimate reasons to talk about situations.* The reporter may ask us *to pray* for the person. The reporter might want to inform us because we are in a position *to help, aid* or *support* him or her. It could be *to get counsel* from us as to how a situation should be handled. Another reason may be to *gain knowledge* or *be educated* about a situation. These are but a few acceptable motivations. Look at the attitude, tonal expressions and facial features; hear not only what is being said but how it is being said. But above all, avoid judging and being condescending in your approach. We have all been caught in patterns of negative conversations. For me, I want someone to help remind me to use words of encouragement and support, not words of destruction.

Will people ever become offended or upset by being asked these questions? Possibly, but if you share with a spirit of love and compassion, it will reduce the chances of someone feeling rejected by your words. Regardless, you cannot take a chance on being party to an evil report. Remember our image of the locomotive; it is much easier to jump off before it starts picking up speed. There are repercussions to sin, and—I cannot stress this enough—*listening to an evil report is a sin.*

We need to control our tongues in order to maintain strong, loving and compassionate relationships with those around us. This is my prayer for all of us:

O Lord, allow our lips to be pure before You. Allow our ears to hear only that which edifies the Body of Christ and keeps us holy. When hearing of misfortune or the "fall" of brothers or sisters, let our desire be to pray for them, to ask Your Holy Spirit to convict them and to restore them. Bring to our minds and to our spirits the strength to turn away from evil and run into Your loving arms. Amen.

EXAMINING THE HEART

1. Do you remember times that you used questions or statements when hearing an evil report? If yes, how did the situation work out?
2. What would be the most difficult part of using the suggested strategies?
3. Would it be easier to use the strategies with a friend or a stranger?

Attitude:
The Cornerstone of Life

Tim and Kathy were wronged. For several days, even weeks, it monopolized their thoughts and conversations. Kathy, however, was able to set the incident aside, put it into perspective and move on with life. Tim, months later, still dwells on the words and actions of the person who wronged them as if the event were yesterday. He is bitter, angry and pessimistic about restoring the relationship in the future.

How is it that two people may experience the same event and the impact upon each person's life is different? Two children raised in the same family, both suffer the tragic and horrible events of abuse. One child is emotionally scarred for many years, unable to develop long-term relationships. This impacts a marriage, jobs and friendships. The other child, also emotionally scarred, is able to overcome this barrier. This person is able to process more effectively, develop relationships that are more permanent, and does not dwell on the pain inflicted by the perpetrator. Even forgiveness comes easier to the second child.

That people respond differently to difficult and painful events is not an earth-shattering revelation. The revelation would be to find "the key to responding effectively in difficult situations." Noted author and speaker Charles Swindoll wrote an interesting piece about our perspectives, specifically about our attitudes.

> The longer I live, the more I realize the impact of attitude on life. Attitude, to me, is more important than facts. It is more important than the past, than education, than money, than circumstances, than failures, than successes, than what other people think or say or do. It is more important than appearance, giftedness, or skill. It will make or break a company . . . a church . . . a home. The remarkable thing is we have a choice every day regarding the attitude we will embrace for that day. We cannot change our past. . . . We cannot change the fact that people will act in a certain way. We cannot change the inevitable. The only thing we can do is play on the one string we have, and that is our attitude. . . . I am convinced that life is 10 percent what happens to me and 90 percent how I react to it. And so it is with you. We are in charge of our attitudes.
>
> Charles Swindoll, *Strengthening Your Grip*

What is attitude? Attitude impacts the way we look at people. Attitude affects whether we make ourselves available to relationships. It impacts our words and speech patterns. An attitude can be positive, negative or even neutral. Let's define some features of this critical attribute and then attempt to capture the essence of this elusive characteristic we call "attitude."

Webster's Ninth New Collegiate Dictionary defines *attitude* as "a mental position, feeling, or an emotion toward a fact or state."

It is clear that attitudes are formed from percepti
experiences and from judgments. Our attitudes ma
based on interactions, new information, moods, illnesses and,
again, experiences. This is why it is so important to be aware of
our critical comments about others, as it will pollute others. A
bad attitude may result in impatience, frustration, withdrawal,
and even anger or aggression, whereas a positive attitude will
often manifest itself with smiles, encouragement, support and
a willingness to extend oneself toward others.

Some years ago, I read *Man's Search for Meaning* by Viktor
Frankl. It had a profound impact on my attitude and perspective
in life. Frankl was a young Austrian Jewish doctor who was a
prisoner in the Auschwitz concentration camp. Everything was
taken from him including his possessions, his family, his lifestyle,
his health and his dignity. However, Frankl states that there was
one thing that could not be taken—his attitude.

Dr. Frankl tells of a time during his imprisonment where
his energy, health, sadness over the death of his family and
perspective on life were at their lowest. On the verge of col-
lapse, almost ready to give up and embrace death, Frankl rose
up in his spirit and refused to allow the Nazis to gain control
of his attitude. When waves of depression came over him, he
imagined standing before thousands of people and sharing his
experiences with them. He visualized himself interacting with
others and impressing upon them the importance of purpose
and destiny. In all his pain, Viktor Frankl's desire was to reach
out and touch humanity to educate them regarding holding on
to one's attitude. He survived the horrors of Auschwitz and his
vision became reality.

His book sold over two million copies and has been quoted
throughout the world. It demonstrates man's inhumanity to
man as well as the power of attitude and choices in life. His
experiences gave him desire to connect and relate to people,

and to not pull back and retreat from relationships. He wrote, "Everything can be taken from a man but one thing: the last of the human freedoms—to choose one's attitude in any circumstances, to choose one's own way."

After reading this book, I asked myself, "What are some barriers to having a positive outlook on life? What prevents us from seeing a bright future? Why do we hesitate to connect with people, to share our inner spirit with them?"

I decided that one major obstacle would be the area of placing blame. It would have been easy for Viktor Frankl to blame the Nazi army for his pain and suffering. And it would have been accurate, yet it could have left Frankl powerless and impotent. How can a person overcome difficult areas of life when all the control and responsibility is placed upon others? What motivation would there be to help others, to develop relationships when our perspective has been tainted with anger, pain and blame?

As a thirteen-year-old Jewish boy, I experienced the custom and tradition of a bar mitzvah. This is a time when a young Jewish boy or girl moves toward adulthood by his or her involvement in a religious ceremony. The young adolescent conducts an entire religious service (singing, sermon, inspirational readings) for approximately 45 to 60 minutes. The local rabbi is present for support and guidance, but the majority of the responsibility falls upon the young teenager.

I mention this experience because the message I spoke to the congregation was one that became a foundation for my life. I vividly recall the title, the major text of the message as well as the impact it has had on my thinking in life. Let me take some time and share the essence of the message and a few poignant aspects. I will deviate from the original text, elaborating, clarifying and emphasizing points when necessary. Though my thirteen-year-old understanding was well beyond my years (more like a fourteen-year-old's), I do believe I now have a greater comprehension of the life lessons and biblical Scriptures, and I have gained personal insights. The title of my sermon from 1968 was "Where Do You Place the Blame?"

Placing Blame

There are four major areas that receive blame for life circumstances not occurring as we planned: other people, family, self, God. It is common for blame to turn into frustration, which may lead to anger and eventually take hold of our lives as bitterness. This bitterness will come forth as negative conversations and attitudes, more often than not. As we explore each area, examine your own life for any roots that may have taken hold and grown into a plant of bitterness.

1. Blaming others (friends, authorities in life, outsiders)

How convenient it is to blame other people for our own failures, lack of responsibility and poor decisions. When the credit card bill is high, I conveniently notice the charges my wife made and selectively overlook my own. When I eat the chocolate cake, even though I am on a diet, yes, you guessed it: "Why did you make this cake, Joyce? It is your fault I broke my diet."

Pointing the finger at other people becomes our first line of defense—diverting attention away from us and creating a need for others to defend their actions. A scriptural example of this is in Exodus. When Moses confronts Aaron about the golden calf, Aaron's response deflects personal responsibility and blames others.

And Moses said to Aaron, "What did this people do to you that you have brought so great a sin upon them?" So Aaron said, "Do not let the anger of my lord become hot. *You know the people, that they are set on evil."*

Exodus 32:21–22, emphasis added

Aaron not only continues to blame the people but also totally absolves himself of any wrongdoing by indicating that the calf was supernaturally made.

And I [Aaron] said to them, "Whoever has any gold, let them break it off." So they gave it to me, and I cast it into the fire, and this calf came out.

Exodus 32:24

Another translation reads,

"Then I asked them to bring me their gold earrings. They took them off and gave them to me. I threw the gold into a fire, and out came this bull."

CEV

What a miracle! The gold was thrown into the fire and a golden calf just jumped out! Although this seems ludicrous, many excuses we use to defend ourselves are often equally ridiculous.

Blaming others is especially easy when the people are not around to defend themselves. The personal connection to the other people makes "blame shifting" easy. Just as Aaron blamed "the people" and hoped relationship with Moses would allow him to get away with shirking responsibility, we can also do the same thing. "You know me. You're my friend. Don't trust those other people. It was their fault, not mine." Our attitude of manipulation and partial truth impact our thinking, and we make attempts to absolve ourselves of responsibility.

I wonder if Aaron would have used the same excuse if he were surrounded by some of the very people he used as a rationale for his behavior. Or if King Saul would have blamed the people while claiming his own obedience in destroying the Amalekites if others were within listening distance (see 1 Kings 15)? Notice a pattern here. We usually justify and rationalize when others are not around to question our conversations.

You can see how easy it would be to fall into the trap of negative conversations and critical comments. This common approach allows for the focus to be on the other person, their faults and their issues. Using gossip as a way to deflect attention and blame is a frequent ploy used by each of us.

Our perspective will impact the way we view life. Noted author Kahlil Gibran wrote, "Your living is determined not so much by what life brings to you as by the attitude you bring to life; not so much by what happens to you as by the way your mind looks at what happens."[1] Are you in control of your attitude or does your attitude control you?

2. Blaming family

When we do not get our own way, it is convenient to blame those closest to you, often family members. When our son was unable to find an article of clothing, it was Mom's fault. True, his room looked like a tornado landed in the midst of the room, but if Mom had put things away, it would not have looked like that. "Why are all these clothes on my bed?" he asked. I suppose the clean laundry could have been placed on the floor, which was somewhere underneath other items. Or, as some of you may be thinking, let him do his own laundry. Well, since he went away to college, that has occurred. That is, except when he comes home for the holidays and brings two suitcases full of dirty clothes. The joys of parenting.

When I am driving and cannot find a specific location, I may blame my wife. If she could only find directions faster on

1. This quote is also frequently credited to John Homer Miller.

MapQuest, get a straight answer from Siri or just stop asking me to get directions from the nearest gas station. After all, I will find the place any minute. Yeah, right! (Thank goodness for a GPS.)

I grew up in a house with three other brothers, none of whom took responsibility for minor household disasters such as broken lamps, holes in doors, lost toys, etc. (While my brothers would now say it was mostly me who created these problems, their selective memory is probably due to their age. Please forgive them, for they know not what they do.) When my father asked who used the hammer without putting it away, my oldest and self-proclaimed best brother, Steve, responded, "Not me." Then, on down the line, Mark, Mike and Marty said in unison, "It wasn't me." Since my mom knew it had not been her, we had a dilemma. No one had done it, yet the deed had been done. We soon had the birth of a new brother, "Mr. Nobody." So whenever something happened, and we all were not to blame, my parents blamed Mr. Nobody. It is still a family joke.

It is easy to blame others—even easier to blame your family. We are aware of the flaws, warts and idiosyncrasies of our siblings, parents and relatives. We have seen them at their worst, and they, in turn, have seen us. That is why it is so difficult for a person to change his or her image within the family. The youngest sibling will always be the baby, regardless of how much he earns, what fame she achieves or how successful he may become in life (sorry, Marty). Family members see one another through the grid of the past. The problem with this approach is that it does not allow people to change or even to grow up.

Family members blame one another out of convenience and due to emotional frustration. Family is an ever-present, easy target. Even in the best of families, tempers flare, frustrations occur and harsh words are spoken. Unfortunately, many families refuse to communicate through these times, and offenses build. The walls of bitterness may prevent relationships from healing and growing. Once again, the use of evil reports becomes commonplace and more walls are erected.

We find an example of family conflict within the Bible. During one particular tirade, King Saul was upset at David. But when Saul's son Jonathan spoke words in David's defense, Saul's anger was directed quickly at his own son, and his rage so overwhelmed him that Saul threw a spear at Jonathan in an attempt to kill him (see 1 Samuel 20:27–33). Anger at David was redirected or displaced toward Jonathan.

As part of my consulting and training work, I travel to speak to schools, businesses and churches. In the schools, the area of blaming family is up-front and personal with educators. After spending a long day with 25 to 35 children in each class, and showing love, compassion and patience that would rival Job's, teachers come home to their own abodes. Ahhhh, home sweet home! But, walking in the door, the parent is met with clothes on the floor and dishes in the sink. The children are arguing at full volume. Suddenly, the paragon of strength and patience turns into a feisty, frustrated pit bull that lashes out at anything in the way. "Who left these clothes on the floor? And why aren't the dishes done? Quit arguing and go to your rooms until dinner. I don't want to hear a peep from anyone."

You see, many of us spend our days mediating, resolving conflicts, attempting to move through life with the least resistance and maximum results. When we get around family, we are hoping for support and some type of soothing atmosphere. But when met with the same problems we faced all day, our frustration soars and we lose our perspective in life.

My wife and I had a disagreement (just one), and she turned to me and said, "Mike, do you just want me to agree with you? Would that make you happy?"

I said, "Yes, it would." I just wanted to have someone agree with me. I did not want to have to persuade and convince her as I had all day with people at work. We both laughed.

3. Blaming oneself

In my counseling experiences, I have found many people who are able to forgive the other person but unable to forgive themselves. Guilt overwhelms them and they become trapped by their own self-doubt, low self-esteem, lack of confidence and shame. "Poor Me" becomes the mantra for this person, and soon he or she is powerless to overcome the personal demons of negativism that invade the mind and spirit.

There is no more powerful example of this than the response by Judas to the betrayal of Jesus. Overcome by personal shame and blame, Judas committed suicide to end his pain (see Matthew 27:5). In contrast, we find Peter, who denied even knowing Jesus (a betrayal of their intimate relationship), yet Peter was able to put his personal failure into perspective, receive forgiveness and become a great leader and apostle to the first-century Church.

In one person, Judas, we see self-incrimination to the point of depression and shame and ultimately death. In the other, Peter, we find a realistic understanding of his own humanity. We must put our own mistakes into perspective, seeing them as areas of growth and not malignant weaknesses. Until we are able to recognize life as a walk of learning and growth, we will continue to beat ourselves up with expectations of perfection, a level that we will never achieve in this life.

Each person should be willing to admit mistakes without becoming trapped in the spiral of guilt, blame and critical conversations. It is okay to be wrong, to make an error. The problem occurs when we refuse to change our actions and the problems become habits. We fall into the cycle of guilt and blame. A sense of shame haunts us, but we become incapable (or unwilling) to change our behaviors. People who are haunted with guilt will find it entangling their relationships and creating ineffectiveness in ministering to other people.

4. Blaming God

"Why me?" is a familiar phrase for many of us when things do not go the way we plan. Our anger and frustration are directed toward God. After all, we do the right things. We follow His commandments the best we can. We pray. We read the Bible. We attend church, yet God seems to have it out for us. Financial struggles, health issues, family problems happen. The life of a faithful believing person should be better, right?"He sends rain on the just and on the unjust" (Matthew 5:45).

Is God to blame for my problems? On one hand, the answer appears to be a definitive and resounding YES! After all, He created me and allowed me to grow and mature in the world. If my life had ended earlier, or if I had never existed, the problems would be a moot point. So to say God is responsible for my problems because He is the author of life would be an accurate statement.

On the other hand, to blame God for my problems only places me in an impotent position. If I am not in control of my life, not able to impact my decisions, not capable of choices, then my life is not really my own. It is this mind-set that leads to blaming others, blaming family and blaming self.

How curious that we are willing to blame God for difficulties, yet lack the faith that He will overcome problems. The book of Job clearly illustrates this contrast of faith in overcoming and succumbing to a defeatist mentality. While Job saw life as a series of possibilities, his wife and friends viewed life in terms of impossibilities. The question is not whether God is responsible for my present situation, but whether I believe God is capable and willing to impact my future situations.

This aspect of blame is not exclusive to those who attend church, temple or a synagogue. Regardless of one's religious inclinations, God receives blame for many of the heartaches, suffering and personal tragedies experienced in life. This becomes an interesting dynamic in one's personal belief system. If we blame God for disasters and difficulties in life, we must then recognize there is a God and He has control over these areas. This creates a dilemma for some people who have refused to admit the existence or authority found within the essence of God. Can we blame Him for a specific situation when we do not acknowledge Him in general situations?

The Bible shares many examples in which people blame God. From Job's family to the Israelites in Egypt to the Pharisees interacting with Jesus, all questioned the power and authority of God. Jonah 4 finds Jonah blaming God for sparing the people of Nineveh, the enemy of Israel. As with Jonah, we often blame God because we do not understand what has happened in our lives, it is not what we desired and we are fearful of the future possibilities.

Practical Applications

Until we are willing to touch other people with kindness and compassion, our lives will lack a true depth of love and meaning. The late Keith Green sang, "It is so hard to see when my eyes are on me." As long as I am focused on Mike, it is difficult to embrace other people into my life. Unless I embrace others, my life will be a series of selfish events that fail to leave a legacy or make a difference.

We cannot touch another life if we are in isolation. We cannot make a positive impact and impression if we are stuck in the cycle of gossip and criticism. Our attitudes, if we allow them, will take us down a track that leads to pain and broken relationships. Or our attitudes can open up doors of encouragement and support to those around us.

Take time to listen to others

We must avoid inserting our own opinions, ideas and perspectives. Really listen. Hear not only the words from others but also the emotions. What is it they are looking for from us? Support, affirmation, guidance, a listening ear, a friend, companionship . . . ? Be willing to ask the person, "What can I do to help?" Direct the conversation away from gossip and negative conversations and more toward restoration and healing.

Ask other people for their opinion

The Bible tells us that "a man who isolates himself seeks his own desire; he rages against all wise judgment" (Proverbs 18:1). Are we willing to hear another person's opinion? By seeking out another idea or strategy, we sometimes find a better way of handling a situation. This person may help us understand a larger life plan, one that God may have for us. We all need someone whom we respect and use as a sounding board for future decisions.

Avoid telling other people what to do

I recognize there are times at work or at home where we need to tell people what to do. But this can become a trap, and soon we relate to people by barking out commands and telling people what to do. As a schoolteacher, I found that I could tell students what to do or find another way to word my request in such a way that they did not feel bullied. Instead of saying, "Get your books out and read fifteen pages, then take the test," I said, "Go ahead and read the fifteen pages in the book, as they will prepare you for the test." As parents, we bark commands at our children and then wonder why they resist. We must find a way to include our children in the decisions so they will more likely support the approach. Whether on the job, in the home or in the community, people like to share in the responsibilities and decisions. Few people like to be told what to do without having options. In this same manner, look for the options given to us by God. The Bible is a book of guidance, one that offers many choices and opportunities to impact lives.

Be a teacher (and learner) in life, not a spectator

Being an armchair coach is easy. We evaluate what happened and suggest alternatives but have no responsibility for the results. We need to get involved with others. Help guide and encourage others. Be willing to invest in a project and in a person's life. Yes, there may be some disappointment along the way, but it is often overcome by the joy and excitement of relationship. As we share our lives, we teach others to be a conduit and connection in life. Lee Iacocca, former CEO of Chrysler Motors, said that there was one word that described a good manager: *decisiveness*. Make a decision, follow it and put forth all your energy into it.

> In a completely rational society . . . the best of us would aspire to be teachers, and the rest of us would have to settle for something less. The job of passing civilization along from one generation to the next ought to be the highest honor anyone could have.
>
> Lee Iacocca, *Where Have All the Leaders Gone?*

Be a teacher of relationships. Help others see the importance of reaching out and connecting with other people. Avoid blaming others, yourself, family or God. Take responsibility for your words and actions—decide to make a change. As did Dr. Viktor Frankl, choose an attitude that embraces people and allows the positive aspects of your life to flow into the world.

In our next chapter, we begin to examine the specific ways we become influenced by negative conversations. As we continue to evaluate our lives, remember to have a heart of compassion and encouragement toward others. Though we speak strongly about the area of evil reports, the purpose is to assist each one of us toward a more positive speech pattern and to reduce the times we listen to critical statements about others.

===== EXAMINING THE HEART =====

1. Look in the mirror. Do you have a positive or negative outlook on life? What would friends or family say?
2. When others have poor attitudes, does it impact your perspective? If so, what can you do to change this?

5

Why Do We Gossip?

The importance of recognizing the subtle defilement of our minds and spirits when listening to an evil report is essential if we are to overcome lifestyles of gossip and murmuring. If we are unable to recognize the potential destruction caused by negative words, we will eventually cause injury to those around us. And, sadly, we often deceive ourselves into believing there was justification for our actions.

There are many reasons we allow our ears to listen to profane words and our eyes to view coarse actions. There may be pressure from colleagues, family or friends. We may feel trapped by circumstances and unable to break the patterns of life. We may be rebellious and make a conscious decision to violate the ways of God. And there are those of us who think we are strong enough to see and hear impure things and not be affected by them.

As I mentioned earlier, we might view an evil report to be something like a locomotive barreling down certain "tracks" that potentially lead to deception. We will begin looking at these tracks in this chapter and the chapters that follow. The first of these, *confusion*, is one of the major reasons that we allow the negative words and actions of an evil report to violate our sense of well-being. Confusion is a major stumbling block to progressing in our walk with Christ. "In thee, O LORD, do I put my trust: let me never be put to confusion" (Psalm 71:1 KJV). In fact, confusion is one of Satan's greatest tools. The more we become confused, the greater the chance we will make foolish decisions and become contaminated. God's desire is for us to increase in knowledge and be wise as we move through life. "The heart of the prudent acquires knowledge, and the ear of the wise seeks knowledge" (Proverbs 18:15).

Here is a working definition:

> **Confusion:** Listening to conflicting voices to such an extent that we become unsure about our own personal belief system.

Our confusion stems from hearing so many differing views that we fight against the authorities and support systems in our lives. In a family, whose voice or voices are of highest authority? The parents'. At work, whose voice is the final authority? The supervisor. In a classroom? The teacher. When we get confused, we begin to fight against this authority in our life and no longer see these people as help or support for us. This is not to say we cannot disagree with those in authority. In fact, there are times we need to speak up and share our views.

In my book *When to Speak Up and When to Shut Up* (Chosen Books, 2003), I address the issue of discriminating between speaking up and silence. I discuss how we can disagree with others (family, supervisors, friends) without creating a defensive posture. When we become confused in our perspective and thoughts, poor choices are made in our speech patterns. This will ultimately create difficulties for ourselves as well as those around us. It is imperative to develop self-management and wisdom to know the times to share our opinions and those times we should keep our ideas to ourselves.

Layers of Confusion

When we enter a state of confusion, we lose sight of what is really important in our lives

My wife, Joyce, and I are the best of friends. We are comfortable sharing our personal dreams and desires with one another. Our marriage is wonderful, and I feel there is no other couple as happy or as blessed in life as we are. (I am not so naïve as to believe that we do not have problems or struggles, but we are committed to working out our issues. Many years ago we agreed that divorce was *not* an option in our marriage. My lovely wife is stuck with me.) Despite our commitment and covenant pledge "to honor, obey, love and encourage," there are times when we become "confused" emotionally and our conversations become negative and contaminating.

My role as a husband is one that, over the years, has involved helping with the laundry, transporting our three sons to activities, providing financial security, helping with homework, maintaining a strong spiritual climate in the house . . . among other areas. Joyce and I are a team, and we work together in life. One area that I have helped with for many years is doing the dishes. On occasion I felt that the family did not do as good a job of cleaning the dishes as they should have done, so I have become the resident dishwasher. This is not a job or chore I resent, but one that I offer to be of help to my wife. There are times, however, when I seem to be doing this satisfying area of servanthood with a tremendous heart of love, but my words begin to contradict my actions. "Why can't you clean the dishes like this?" or "If you just rinse off all the soap it is so much simpler." Because I lose a sense of what is really important, I place a barrier between us and injure our relationship. This is especially true when there are other people around to hear my words of "encouragement." Praise God for His forgiveness and grace over my insensitive nature! And I am grateful for a wife who also forgives my foot-in-mouth tendencies.

Confusion blinds us. We begin to say negative comments that cause injury to those around us. Our insensitivity is seen in our lack of discriminating between when to say something and when to keep our mouths shut. Instead of sitting down with my wife and sharing privately the concerns I may have, I have used public opportunities to slander and injure the one I love. We must not let confusion taint our focus; ill-spoken words can cause serious damage to relationships.

Confusion has an impact on those around us and creates disorder in life

This infectious nature of confusion is seen in the story of Gideon destroying the Midianites and Amalekites (see Judges 7). Gideon and his three hundred men were strategically placed around the camp of the enemy.

> Now the Midianites and Amalekites, all the people of the East, were lying in the valley as numerous as locusts; and their camels were without number, as the sand by the seashore in multitude. . . . Then [Gideon] divided the three hundred men into three companies, and he put a trumpet into every man's hand, with empty pitchers, and torches inside the pitchers.
>
> Judges 7:12, 16

The army of God waited for the signal from Gideon. Then they blew their trumpets, broke the pitchers, shouted out a war cry and held up torches. The Bible tells us the enemies of God were so confused by this they began to attack one another. So great was the disorder and disunity that the Midianites and Amalekites killed one another. Imagine it. One person yells, "What is going on?" Another soldier shouts, "Look out, I see torches and hear the horns of battle!" One soldier sees a sword being drawn in the dark of night. The glint of the moonlight off the sharp edge of the sword quickens his pulse. He must defend himself! "What is happening? Why is there so much noise? Those trumpets are so loud, the torches coming at us. . . . I need to attack before I am slain!" Quickly, without hesitation, he thrusts his sword into the nearest person. Within a moment, the soldiers are fighting shadows and movements. Get the picture? It is pretty easy to see how this confusion becomes rampant in the camp of the enemy.

It is exactly like this in our lives. When we become confused, we allow our own thoughts and feelings to be influenced by those around us. It has been said that we are known by the company we keep. If we surround ourselves with people who are seeking God, walking in an upright manner, our lives will reflect this condition. If we keep company with those who gossip, murmur and are discontent, our spirits will be defiled and we will be a reflection of these attitudes.

It is particularly imperative when one is counseling, evangelizing, discipling or participating in any other type of ministry to put on the armor of God. Whenever I pray or counsel with someone in the area of deliverance from addictions or strong emotional bondages and patterns, I always pray a cleansing prayer over all of those involved in the prayer time. The nature of confusion is too easily imparted to one another.

If this sounds odd to you, take a moment and remember the last time you were around someone who was really angry and verbally or physically aggressive. Did you notice the increase in adrenaline in your body? How about your thought process? Did you find your mind going over what you should have said or what you could have done? Now, imagine coming into contact with a friend or family member soon afterward. Where are your thoughts, your emotions? Still caught up in the recent assaultive words and actions? This is what I mean by being confused and needing to be cleansed.

This is especially true when a situation is stressful or volatile. For you sports fans, this can be likened to the end of a football game when players are unsure what play is to be run, the coaching staff is confused and the result is most assuredly defeat. Or think about the political front. Those in political office often attribute errors in statements and decisions to confusion among their staff, political antagonists or the general public. Confusion leads to conflicting statements, and it becomes almost impossible to decipher truth from deception. Confusion opens up our bodies, souls and spirits to be influenced by the environment around us.

A young woman called my office one day and asked to meet with me regarding some dreams and nightmares that had tormented her for weeks. My wife and I met with her, and she shared a series of bizarre events in her life that impacted her current emotional and mental state. We listened, gave counsel and then prayed over her for quite some time. Honestly, it was a rather strange situation. While my wife and I felt confident in our prayers and the authority that God has given to all of us (see Mark 16), this particular time of counsel and prayer was filled with confusion and disjointed thoughts.

That night, both Joyce and I felt discouraged, weighted down with emotions and a general sense of lethargy. As we talked, we realized that the earlier events were still impacting us. We spent time talking and in prayer and soon felt this oppression lift from us. Again, this is not an uncommon occurrence. When you work with people, there will be many an attitude that will be passed along to others. Be careful not to take on another person's offense, attitude of jealousy or complaining nature.

In 1977 I became a Christian. I moved to a small town in the Northwest, where I was part of a service organization offering support to single-parent families, at-risk youth and families in financial stress. My desire to serve and help others was great, but my foundation of servanthood was weak. I became friends with a young man named Tom. He and I would play basketball together, go to movies and "hang out." Part of hanging out with Tom included going to the bars to drink beer. I was a new Christian and still had many "marks of the world" on me. I had not placed myself in a position of being discipled by a godly person, nor was I involved in accountability with other Christian brothers, so I was unsure in many foundational areas of Christianity. I accompanied Tom to the bar and inevitably spent time drinking—many times drinking too much.

After some time, God showed me the poor testimony this presented to those around me. I was known as Tom's drinking buddy, not as a man who loved God. This type of compromise is common among the Christian community.

I am not speaking about the issue of drinking. That is a personal decision. However, I am talking about my decision to drink with Tom as it was easier to "go with the flow" rather than take a stand in my own lifestyle. My confusion came from wanting acceptance from Tom and his friends at the same time I wanted to take a different road in life, one that moved me closer to God.

I do not blame Tom for what happened. This was my error and my poor judgment. A lack of discipline and the failure to place myself under godly headship resulted in my wanting to touch the Spirit of God *and* the spirits (pun intended) of the world. Due to the lack of strong accountability and discipling, my testimony and impact in that town were minimal. Sadly enough, people would only remember me as a guy who would go to the bars, listen to crude jokes and drink too many beers.

It was readily apparent to me in subsequent years that God wanted me to be a pure vessel for Him to use. My confusion was due to immaturity and a lack of teaching from godly men and women; nonetheless, I had a negative influence during that time in my life. There may have been some who wanted to know more about God and looked to me as a role model. I am sure that they, in turn, became confused by my incongruent actions and words. I have prayed many times for God to make my crooked paths straight. "For God is not the author of confusion but of peace, as in all the churches of the saints" (1 Corinthians 14:33).

Confusion creates a need for acceptance from those around us

We want to be loved, accepted and seen as part of the crowd. This is part of the fallen nature of *every* person. Due to this, we tend to listen to conversations we should not hear and to say things that are detrimental to us and those around us. James 3:6 tells us: "And the tongue is a fire, a world of iniquity. The tongue is so set among our members that it defiles the whole body. . . ." All around us are examples of people speaking gossip and slander and giving evil reports about their spouses, friends, supervisors and neighbors. No wonder we get so confused by these negative comments!

We must be wary of conversations that appear to lean toward mocking and putting people down. Think back to the last time you heard something negative about a person. Who shared it with you? Most likely it was someone considered in close relationship. As we become more immersed in the layers of confusion, our filtering process (discernment) begins to minimize. Soon we are listening to conversations that weeks before we would have walked away from due to their content.

We must begin to walk and act maturely, separating ourselves from conversations that bring pain and destruction. Shake off this level of confusion; see and understand who the people are who tend to defile others by their conversation. These are not the people we need to be around when we are vulnerable and impressionable.

There are those who have a strong tendency toward mercy. This can translate into the erroneous belief that being merciful means not confronting. One may interpret mercy as avoiding challenging someone because it might hurt his feelings; stopping a conversation or refusing to listen might be rude. No, I will tell you what is rude. It is rude to knowingly be a part of gossip. It is not good manners to listen to verbal assaults and blatant character assassinations of people who are not present to defend themselves. It is foolishness and ignorance. We must open our eyes and discern when we are listening to evil reports in order to be accepted by the crowd.

Confusion can camouflage the speaker's true intentions and what motivates his evil report

The following list of underlying motivations for giving an evil report is not meant to be exhaustive. There are certainly more than ten motivations that may lead to impure hearts. If you think of others, add them to this list and investigate ways to prevent them from having an impact on your life. This list should, however, give you some insight and understanding as to why an individual might knowingly or unknowingly use the weapon of gossip and criticism to attack another person.

ANGER

The emotion of anger can be fueled by any number of situations. Once someone allows anger to consume him, all else seems insignificant. Relationships, appearances, what others think or say—all become diminished in the explosion of anger. Anyone who is overcome by the intensity of rage no longer thinks logically. He enters the affective realm (emotional state) and does not operate in the cognitive realm (thinking state). All of us find it common to say and do things that later we wish we had not said or done. (Do I hear an amen?) Yet the Bible says, "Let all bitterness, wrath, anger, clamor, and evil speaking be put away from you, with all malice" (Ephesians 4:31).

BITTERNESS

When someone reacts out of personal hurt and rejection, the area of bitterness is involved (see Ephesians 4:31 above). Acts 8:23 gives us insight: "For I see that you are poisoned by bitterness." Bitterness can easily lead to a desire for payback. "I want to get back at them for what they did" or "I'll get even" become common phrases in the minds of bitter people. In other words, *revenge*. You may have heard this statement used in jest: "I don't get mad, I get even." This is the motto of the bitter person.

MOCKING

Evil reports may be motivated by a spirit of mockery, making fun of others or putting people down. "Do not be deceived, God is not mocked; for whatever a man sows, that he will also reap" (Galatians 6:7). Someone who mocks others is causing injury or pain to them emotionally. The mocking spirit was found in the Pharisees and in the enemies of Israel and is in the world today. The Bible says that those who sow mocking words into the world, into relationships, will find that same spirit reaped in them.

DECEIT

It becomes commonplace for deceitful people to believe that giving an evil report is perfectly acceptable. They convince themselves that others deserve whatever fate befalls them and that it is okay to help fate along. "For from within, out of the heart of men, proceed evil thoughts . . . wickedness, deceit" (Mark 7:21–22). Deceit is like a blinder—the kind that horses may need to wear to keep their focus forward or in one direction. Those caught by deception can see only one way: *their* way. This leads to misunderstanding, stubbornness and a refusal to learn and to be teachable.

ENVY

Jealousy and envy have at their roots a desire for what other people have in their lives. God has blessed each one of us. Anyone who feels shortchanged need only ask the Lord to reveal those precious gems he does not see in his own life. He does not realize that there is probably someone who feels envious of his talents. How odd that people spend so much time and energy coveting what is not theirs and so little time and energy cultivating what is given to them by God! No one needs what others have; rather, we all need to appreciate what God has given us. "A sound heart is life to the body, but envy is rottenness to the bones" (Proverbs 14:30). Don't covet! Cultivate!

SELF-SEEKING

When a person's *own* priorities, *own* desires, *own* wants and *own* ambitions become more important than seeking God's direction, he or she has become self-absorbed and self-seeking. I know there have been times when I have placed God on the throne of my life. I also know there have been times when I have taken Him off that throne. I do not want *my* mind and soul to make decisions. Inevitably, those decisions do not prove to be fruitful. When *my* will prevails, no one knows how it will turn out. "For where envy and *self-seeking* exist, confusion and every evil thing are there" (James 3:16, emphasis added).

GUILT

When someone attempts to justify past actions, mistakes and attitudes, he can be motivated by guilt to give an evil report. It is apparent that he has made an error, but he is unwilling to admit the mistake. Rather, he covers it up by slandering another person. He cannot recognize that everyone makes mistakes—including him. We all are sinners saved by grace. "For whoever shall keep the whole law, and yet stumble in one point, he is *guilty* of all" (James 2:10, emphasis added). Imagine that I am baking a cake, measuring out every ingredient perfectly. But during the process, I leave out the baking powder or I bake it too long. No matter how perfectly I do the rest of the cake-baking process, the entire cake is ruined. The only recourse is to start over. In life those plagued by guilt must ask for forgiveness and begin to rebuild the relationship again.

OFFENSES

Being offended and holding in hurts and bitterness will lead to evil speaking. Truly, if someone becomes upset with another and offended, it becomes his or her sin. God has commanded us to love our neighbors, to love our enemies, to submit to one another. There is no place for becoming offended. Offenses separate us from God. "Woe to the world because of *offenses*! For offenses must come, but woe to that man by whom the offense comes!" (Matthew 18:7, emphasis added).

REBELLION

Slipping into rebellion makes it easy to justify an independent spirit. Someone who has violated the Holy Spirit and His intent for his life can either repent or rebel. Unfortunately, there are those who choose rebellion. "For rebellion is as the sin of witchcraft, and stubbornness is as iniquity and idolatry" (1 Samuel 15:23). Jezebel is an excellent (or, rather, I should say poor) example of one who felt justified to operate outside of the realm of God's will. In 1 Kings 18 we read of Jezebel, wife of King Ahab, cutting off and killing the prophets of the Lord. The envious, jealous and ungodly nature of Jezebel is revealed in 1 Kings 21. Naboth owned a vineyard next to the palace of King Ahab. The king asked to buy or trade vineyards with Naboth, as it would be convenient for the king to own the vineyard next to his palace. Naboth respectfully declined, as the vineyard was an inheritance and had sentimental value. When Jezebel heard about this, she was undaunted. She simply set up false accusations against Naboth and had him killed. According to people in rebellion, laws, rules and guidelines are for others. Rebels violate people verbally, physically and emotionally. Be careful: Rebellion is a sinister companion, and it can turn a kind, gentle spirit into one that is cruel and insensitive.

PRIDE

The motivation of pride leads to self-exaltation, rather than serving and preferring others. This is commonly demonstrated by those who put others down in order to build themselves up. "Pride goes before destruction, and a haughty spirit before a fall" (Proverbs 16:18). Someone who operates in pride is, in effect, telling Jesus to move off the throne of his or her life.

If we can begin to grasp the foundational motivations of people who speak evil, we can prevent our lives from being defiled by listening to the evil report. Yes, it does take self-control; it does take a willingness to be accountable to others; it does require each one of us to seek God for our own personal areas of sin. And, please, let's remember that we also fall into the above traps and motivations. Perhaps the list can help each one of us short-circuit negative communication patterns in life.

Confusion distorts our perception of how detrimental it is to listen to gossip and murmuring

That is, we find that we enjoy hearing gossip because it exalts us. Gossip tears down those we dislike, those we are jealous or envious of or those we desire to see hurt because they have hurt us.

The time is coming when people won't listen to good teaching. Instead, they will look for teachers who will please them by telling them only what they are itching to hear. They will turn from the truth and eagerly listen to senseless stories.

2 Timothy 4:3–4 CEV

Those who are drawn to gossip and slander have set themselves toward listening to senseless and foolish stories.

The more we listen to slander and talebearing, the more we become callous to its impact on our lives. This is the same for many other areas of life. If we watch violent movies or fill our thoughts with pornography and lust, we become desensitized to the sin.

Our parameters and boundaries become stretched. One beer becomes two, then three, then a six-pack a night. A movie with some questionable content allows us to rationalize watching a movie with explicit sexual content. The more we expose ourselves to negative comments, sinful speech and acts of character defamation, the more likely we will be to become actively involved in these same areas. The nature of sin is this: It always takes you further than you wanted to go, it costs more than you wanted to pay and it keeps you longer than you wanted to stay. It is a road we should not go down, for once we do, it is easy to get lost and takes a long time to get home.

What we need is a way to prevent us from going down this road. A Jewish publication had an advertisement where a stern picture of a rabbi was displayed. At the bottom of the page was an 800 number or "hotline" to call if you had any information you wanted to share about someone's life. The phone call was answered by a rabbi who would tell you whether the information was considered gossip or whether it was okay to share with others. Rather creative and ingenious, yes? I guess instead of a Dear Abby, it was a Dear Rabbi.

Confusion blinds us to how Satan uses evil reports

What may seem to be an innocent discussion among friends may be used by the enemy to create multiple problems in the Kingdom of God.

> For we do not wrestle against flesh and blood, but against principalities, against powers, against the rulers of the darkness of this age, against spiritual hosts of wickedness in the heavenly places.
>
> Ephesians 6:12

Our involvement in ungodly conversation will affect every area of our lives. It is impossible to isolate the cancer of sin from infecting the entire body. There are five main areas that seem to be regularly attacked when people are involved in evil reports.

1. Satan will use an evil report to destroy families

Satan can, and will, gain an advantage over each one of us if we are confused and ignorant of his ways. We must be aware of the destructive powers involved in listening to a distorted, untrue or evil word. When people follow a path of confusion, it allows them to fall prey to many deceptive situations. They can be taken advantage of financially, physically and emotionally. Confusion should not be an excuse for our failures. The Bible is clear about evil reports. It also commands us to be wise and not have our heads in the sand regarding Satan's evil ways, "lest Satan should take advantage of us; for we are not ignorant of his devices" (2 Corinthians 2:11).

One of his devices is clearly the use of confusion in our lives. Through prayer, accountability and reading the Word of God, we must keep our minds clear and focused on the truth of God.

2. Satan Uses Evil Reports to Attack Spiritual Leaders and Undermine Their Authority in the Church and the Kingdom of God

A non-supporting comment such as, "Can you believe how strongly the pastor spoke about marriage? It isn't as if he doesn't have his own problems," becomes misconstrued and now forms a weapon of Satan to bludgeon the pastor and his family. "I heard the pastor is having marriage problems" begins to filter through the congregation.

It is astonishing how often negative reports are directed at leadership, and not just spiritual leaders but leaders in general. This may be found in a school setting, a business, a corporation or at the forefront of our political arena. Seldom is there an attack against someone who lacks vision or who is without direction. However, fill a leader's heart with purpose, let him speak of a calling on his life and suddenly attacks abound.

3. Satan May Use a False Report to Create an Atmosphere That Separates Brother from Brother and Sister from Sister

In 2 Samuel, we find the story of Mephibosheth, son of Jonathan. King David wanted to honor those who were in the house of Saul, any offspring of Jonathan, as a way of continuing his covenant with Jonathan (see 2 Samuel 9). The servant of Jonathan, Ziba, was jealous and attempted to separate the heart of David from Mephibosheth (see 2 Samuel 16:1–4). Because of Ziba's lies and deception, King David thought Mephibosheth was out to reclaim the kingdom and overthrow him. Nothing was ever substantiated. David was only going on what Ziba had stated, which was an evil report. He then took away all that was given to Mephibosheth and gave it to Ziba. In 2 Samuel 19 we find David and Mephibosheth confronting one another.

> The king said to him, "Why did you not go with me, Mephibosheth?" And he answered, "My lord, O king, my servant deceived me. For your servant said, 'I will saddle a donkey for myself, that I may ride on it and go to the king,' because your servant is lame. And [Ziba] has slandered your servant to my lord the king."
>
> verses 25–27

Once David realized that he had listened to an evil report, he corrected his error and blessed Mephibosheth. He also divided the land between Mephibosheth and his servant. Satan's desire is to separate God's people from one another and to create a barrier between the people and their God-given leaders.

4. SATAN DESIRES TO DIVIDE AND CONQUER

The Bible tells us that God is not the author of confusion (see 1 Corinthians 14:33). If it is not God, then it must be Satan, Lucifer, Slewfoot. We have an enemy, and his job is to "steal, and to kill, and to destroy" (John 10:10). Satan is "seeking whom he may devour" (1 Peter 5:8). Satan and all his demonic forces do not want unity among Christians; they do not want unity between people of different faiths, beliefs and cultures; they do not want unity among churches and the various religious organizations; they certainly do not want peace to reign in our lives. Each and every evil report will be twisted and turned to the benefit of God's enemies. What side of the fence do you fall on?

5. SATAN USES EVIL REPORTS TO BELITTLE GOD'S PEOPLE

How many newspaper headlines have decried the work of a godly person? *Right-wing religious fanatics, ultraconservative legalists, narrow-minded zealots*—these are just a few of the headlines depicting Christians. I understand that people who have legally or morally sinned need to be held accountable for their inappropriate and ungodly actions. However, the way some are vilified and castigated is contrary to God's way. And, sadly, this is true within the Christian community as well. The Body of Christ (the Church at large) should be a testimony of prayer, of compassion and of restoration. When a person falls into a sinful pattern, our greatest desire should be for restoration not consequences, for repentance not persecution, for humility not embarrassment. What are we modeling to the unbeliever? Our approach and response to sin and failure should be a source of encouragement and strength to unbelievers.

As we conclude this section, be aware of any areas in which God has convicted you about confusion leading to gossip in your life. Take time and repent. Allow God to cleanse your heart, purify your spirit from defilement and guide your tongue in future conversations. We can have our habits changed by the intervention of the Holy Spirit and feel free from mental captivity. We are not bound by our past mistakes. We must make it our primary desire to seek His Kingdom and His righteousness.

EXAMINING THE HEART

1. When you are confused, how do you respond to people around you? Do you attack? Do you become defensive? Overly critical? Overly sensitive?

2. In your personal life, what can you do to prevent becoming bound by confusion?

6

Keeping Free from Verbal Contamination

Prior to entering full-time pastoral ministry, I worked for fifteen years in the public school setting. My roles included director of special education, social worker/counselor and, for my final six years, classroom teacher. It was during my time as an educator that I experienced (and participated in) a saturation of evil reports. The teachers' lounge is a dangerous place if you want to avoid negative discussions.

Do not misunderstand: I am not suggesting that all schools are a haven for evil reports, though many would probably qualify for an A in Rumor Mill 101! I am stating, however, that the world is a conglomeration of people, many of whom lack understanding of the danger of gossip and spreading rumors. This is true for many businesses in both the private and public sectors. Since many years of my experience occurred in the public school system, my illustrations naturally are drawn from that setting.

Behind Closed Doors

The teachers' lounge is a place for educators to sit and talk without a student or parent present. Most schools have a no-admittance policy for students or, at the least, require that they knock on the lounge door and wait outside for a response. This carefully constructed off-limits sector provides the opportunity to talk about people without fear of being overheard.

In my experience, it was not uncommon for an educator to speak negatively about a student or parent only to have someone else chime in with similar frustrations. As the feeding frenzy continued, this unsuspecting student or parent was "filleted" unmercifully. It seemed that as these discussions continued, the educator became more and more bitter toward the student or parent. The anger increased, and soon a rationale for punishment or retreating emotionally was born. "As surely as rain blows in from the north, anger is caused by cruel words" (Proverbs 25:23 CEV).

We might be tempted to excuse the conversation. After all, this was in a private setting. Furthermore:

- What if the comments were accurate?
- Didn't the educators involved share situations that actually occurred?
- Isn't it okay just to vent and receive moral support?

It does not matter if the statements are accurate. When an individual attempts to defame another person's character through negative comments, we have an evil report in the making. The Bible states clearly that gossip and cruel words only create more strife. And the issue of moral support? If a person is sharing frustration in order to receive counsel for future interactions, we have a different scenario. Most situations, though, reveal stories and gossip being used to elicit support and sympathy for the gossip, *not to cover and aid the victim*. The attempt at restoration is seldom seen within the confines of these private walls.

As I mentioned, a teachers' lounge is not the only place where people speak negatively of others. Your workplace may have a staff lounge, a lunchroom or a designated area where groups gather each day. In a church the temptation to murmur is before us constantly at gatherings like choir rehearsals or board meetings. In a home, one might use the living or family room to entertain people (with gossip). We certainly use the telephone, texting, Twitter, Facebook and other social media as channels for our negative expressions toward others. And don't get me started on reality shows!

Begin to identify the places where gossip and rumors prevail in your life. Set up an action plan to avoid or minimize your involvement. Share this plan with another and hold yourself accountable. Minimizing gossip will definitely decrease the anger and frustration in the lives of people who are normally touched by it. "Where there is no fuel a fire goes out; where there is no gossip arguments come to an end. Troublemakers start trouble, just as sparks and fuel start a fire" (Proverbs 26:20–21 CEV). We can change habits and therefore help change the patterns of those we come in contact with each day.

The Track of Contamination

What if we are in situations that do not allow us to leave easily? Can we just be quiet and say nothing?

No, and here is the reason why not: We run the risk of moving on to the next track toward deception, which is spiritual *contamination*. Here is a definition:

Contamination: Allowing one's spirit to be polluted through negative conversation.

The tracks being presented throughout this book are somewhat hierarchical in nature. That is, if we are in a state of *confusion* as to what is occurring, we will have a tendency to become involved in the conversation, which leads to the *contamination* of our spirits. Each track will slowly and methodically lead us into the depths of defilement. Each, however, has a biblical and practical antidote, if you will, that will help us avoid the snare of the enemy.

Imagine we are in a factory, wandering around inspecting and investigating the contents of the work area. There is a large sign on one door: Do Not Enter—Contamination. It is safe to assume that we would not glibly enter that room knowing it is almost certainly a danger to our lives. What if there were no sign? What if, during our inspection, we found ourselves in the midst of a contaminated room exposed to radioactive materials? We would flee the area and get medical attention.

The next time we go to inspect that factory, we most certainly will not let ourselves be led into an unsafe area of contamination again. Why do we, then, continue to place ourselves in situations where we constantly become contaminated by unhealthy and ungodly language, discussions and conversations? The pollution from these conversations is every bit as deadly (to our mental and emotional state) as that of radioactive materials (to our physical state). Our lives will be filled with pain and suffering, and our words will have a tremendous impact on those around us.

Why Silence Does Not Get the Message Across

Let me explain why there often needs to be a response, either verbally or physically (such as leaving the area if that is an option). I recently received a phone call from a telephone solicitor. Naturally, the call came at a most inconvenient time. The individual on the phone began with the usual greeting, "How are you tonight, Mr. Sedler?" Inwardly, I knew where this might be heading, but I responded, as usual, with a chatty "Fine, thank you." The voice went on to say, "Would you like to improve the quality of your relationship with your wife?"

This was a loaded question. If I said no, it might appear as though I did not care about my wife. I began to waver. What if this was not a solicitor at all? I became irrational. Maybe Joyce was testing me. Perhaps it was someone from church who had been through our marriage classes and was seeing if I really "walk the walk." Oh! The pressure was mounting. In a moment of weakness and foolishness, I responded as many people would, "I have a good relationship with my wife, but of course, it could be better."

That was all it took; the first fine threads of the spider's web were wrapping around me.

The person continued with his persuasive speech and for the next several minutes took control of the conversation, telling me about a magazine that would supposedly enhance every facet of our relationship. I waited for him to take a breath so I could respond, but he must have been connected to an oxygen tank! I listened casually, with the opportunity for only an occasional "Yes . . . uh-huh . . ." and a few nods of the head (as if that were discernible over the phone). As the salesperson wound down his monologue and I was ready to interject, "No, thank you," he took a turn that caused me to stutter and stumble verbally again. The salesperson concluded his sales pitch with this comment, "Now, Mr. Sedler, do you have a credit card?" I could not seem to stop myself. The web was getting thicker. I replied with a terse, "Yes."

He continued, "Well, Mr. Sedler, we can bill you and have you pay $29.99 by check for a one-year subscription, or you can use your credit card and pay $24.99 for one year. Which would you like?" This was not going as I planned. My response of

"No, thank you" did not fit into the options I was given. And besides, did he really think I would not have chosen the credit card to save the five dollars? (You can see that the web had gotten strong indeed!)

After several awkward minutes and some gentle combat, I hung up the phone. I was frustrated at the time I had wasted, but even more uptight over what I felt was the audacity of the salesperson to assume I wanted his magazine. I discovered later that I was looking at this from the wrong angle.

Some time after this phone call, I was talking with a friend who, during the course of our conversation, explained a term that helped me understand the approach of the magazine solicitor. It also helped me to see the importance of responding and not just sitting silently listening to an evil report. (I am referring here, of course, to ungodly conversations, not suggesting that calls from solicitors are ungodly.) My friend explained that in the business realm, there is a term called *implied consent*. Many salespeople use this as a ploy to get customers to buy from them. The tone of the conversation is always focused on the sale of the merchandise. It is assumed that the person will buy the product, and all discussion is geared toward making the sale as compatible for the consumer as possible. My silence was allowing the salesperson to weave a large web around me. In business terms, my silence was implying that I consented to buy the product. If you are in the sales field, do not be alarmed by my analogy. The person who called did nothing wrong. He was polite, but persuasive. If I had responded in a disinterested fashion sooner, the conversation would have ended more quickly. The point is that this applies to carriers of evil reports. The sooner I respond in a contrary way, the quicker the conversation will end. Are you involved in implied consent with those who are sharing an evil report?

Let me share another story that shows the power of using my words. We were attending a time-share sales pitch (that in itself should say enough about the setting). We received a three-night vacation, but agreed to a ninety-minute presentation. We indicated, up front, that we were not interested, but we were assured that we could simply enjoy the three-night vacation without having to buy anything. As the salesperson moved along with the presentation, the pressure began to build. One could feel the crescendo coming, when a decision would be asked of Joyce and me. When the person gave us his closing pitch, I calmly stated that we were committed elsewhere with our finances. He assured me the monthly payments would be low and affordable. I agreed that they seemed very reasonable, but our money was going toward putting our son through college and any extra money would be used for the next child. Though he persisted, I stayed the course and even asked at one point, "Are you asking me to spend my son's education money on a time-share?" This caught him off guard and reduced the pressure to buy immensely. A polite but firm approach kept the discussion within an acceptable realm. Silence would only have encouraged more discussion.

Speaking Boldly

Then the question arises: If we understand the negative consequences of listening to the conversation, if silence is not an option, if our spirits are more in danger of contamination the longer we listen to an evil report, what is the next step?

The next step is to speak boldly. Let me give two examples that help show how to put this into practice.

The first example gives an effective response for use in a large group setting. I have not always had the freedom, nor have I always desired, to leave the room where gossip was occurring. Once I became aware of the impact it was having on my spirit and my attitude, however, I found this approach effective. Sometimes the best way to negate gossip in a group discussion is to join in on the conversation. (What? Join the negative discussions? Stay with me for a few more sentences.) One thing you will notice is that these discussions are open to anybody, especially those who fuel the fire. My comments, however, are intended to *throw water on the fire, not gasoline.*

For instance, suppose a fellow teacher says something like this: "Jimmy is such a frustration. He never gets his work done and he is so lazy." (As you can see, this statement has no merit toward restoration with Jimmy. It is only meant to gain sympathy or support for the person speaking the assertions.) My response might be something like this: "I also have Jimmy in class. Have you noticed the last week or so his work is really improving?" If the person answers with a negative or flippant response, "No, I think he is getting worse," I, again, respond with a positive, "Maybe he does better for me because I have him in the morning" or "He is doing better for me; I hope it will carry over." A bold positive response can put out the fire.

And the second example will help you in one-on-one conversations. Imagine you are at a friend's house and he or she begins to speak negatively about his or her spouse. This is, unfortunately, very common. "My spouse is driving me crazy. He/she is so inconsiderate and selfish sometimes. I can hardly stand to be around the person." While this comment is born out of hurt and frustration, it can be the beginning of a complaining and grumbling spirit. Instead of asking the person to give you more details, minimize the damage of an evil report with a comment like this: "It sounds as if you are really hurting. What can I do to help you?" After the response you may reply, "I am going to commit to pray each day for your marriage. I know God has a destiny and plan for both of you. In fact, let's pray now."

If the person is a non-Christian, you can still respond in a way that circumvents further negative discussion. "It sounds as if you are really hurting. Marriage really takes a lot of work and can be a bit overwhelming at times. I'm sure if you need some guidance there are good counselors available. I will certainly be praying for you." Prayer and encouragement can also douse the flames of a negative conversation.

These types of positive approaches shut down the tendency for others to add additional negative comments. It is a funny (or perhaps sad) thing about evil reports: Our carnal nature desires to touch and to entertain them. We are not usually repulsed by these conversations. In fact, many times we are lured into them by the enticing aroma and taste of sin. It is true that many of us like to be in the midst of conversations and "in the know," but the remnant of such discussions is often sorrow and pain. "The words of a talebearer are as wounds, and they go down into the innermost parts of the belly" (Proverbs 18:8 KJV).

I realize that speaking boldly against murmuring and gossip is not easy to do and can make for awkward moments. There are some of us who do not feel comfortable confronting situations and hope and pray those situations will simply disappear. "If I just don't say anything, they will get the idea I am not a part of their discussion and not interested in their opinions" is often the reasoning, but it does not help in the event of an evil report.

There have certainly been occasions when I did not say anything, which allowed someone to continue to speak inappropriately of another. I am a man-pleaser at times. I fear the responses of certain people. There have been times when I should have left the room, made a contrary statement (a positive comment) or asked for further clarification. My unwillingness to intervene was due to my carnal nature. This is not an excuse but simply a confession of my inadequacies and my lack of strength in certain situations.

When a Proud Heart Is the Issue

So far in this chapter we have looked at a few ways to diffuse or minimize a negative report. We can see that it is possible, even though it may take courage. We have seen the importance of speaking, but speaking sensitively and with encouragement. But what if we fail to do so? What if we willingly listen to negative talk? What if we know what is happening, but we refuse time and again to stop it?

This is an important issue to God. His Word consistently and repeatedly draws our attention to it. He clearly tells us what will happen to those involved in spreading negative reports—and remember that condoning them by silence is tantamount to spreading them. "Whoever secretly slanders his neighbor, him I will destroy; the one who has a haughty look and proud heart, him I will not endure" (Psalm 101:5). Another translation says, "Anyone who spreads gossip will be silenced; no one who is conceited will be my friend" (CEV). What is God referring to when He says, "The one who has a haughty look and proud heart, him I will not endure," or "No one who is conceited will be my friend"?

I see a person with a "proud heart" or an individual with blatant "conceit" as one who feels he can do whatever he desires. This person's arrogance allows him to believe he is above God's laws and, supposedly, will receive no repercussions for vain choices. Perhaps this would be a person who believes he can associate with carriers of evil reports, surround himself with ungodly conversations, subject himself to crude discussions and emerge unscathed. After all, "I can handle it" and "It won't affect me" have been said by those who, eventually, are drawn into total contamination and exposure in their spirits. How about you? Have you said or thought these phrases, believing that you would be exempt from contamination?

My intent is to encourage each of us toward carefully examining our listening habits. My hope is for each of us to be more aware of those times of "contamination" and to reduce being a victim of these situations. Though I do paint a serious picture of listening to evil reports, my purpose is not to "scare you clean." If that worked, I would be gleaming and shiny. However, if we can remember some of these key points, we will increase the likelihood that our lives will be less polluted by critical and negative comments.

The Spiritual Lines of Defense

Physically, we have been equipped with warning systems to prevent contamination from our surroundings. We can tell if the air around us is foul with contaminants by the *sense of smell*. We can detect dangerous surroundings by the *sense of sight*. The *sense of touch* gives us a warning if something is too hot or too sharp. The *sense of taste* warns us if food is rancid. Finally, we become aware of noise pollution by the *sense of hearing*. These five physical senses are warning systems to protect us from potentially dangerous and defiling circumstances.

In the same way, God has provided us with protective spiritual defenses that warn us of spiritual contamination. While these spiritual defenses may utilize the five physical senses to enhance their perception, they operate in a different and independent realm. Here are a few examples of these spiritual defenses that God has made available to us:

1. **Discernment**—Through the gift of the Holy Spirit (see 1 Corinthians 12:10) we have the ability to:
   - discern between good and evil (see 2 Samuel 14:17; 1 Kings 3:9; Hebrews 5:14);
   - discern the thoughts and intents of the heart (see Hebrews 4:12);

- discern between the righteous and the wicked (see Malachi 3:18).

2. **Wisdom**—Through the gift of the Holy Spirit (see 1 Corinthians 12:8) we are able to:

    - receive wisdom from God (see Proverbs 2:6; James 1:5);

    - receive a pure, peaceable wisdom with good fruits and without hypocrisy (see James 3:17);

    - receive wisdom, a more precious gift than gold (see Proverbs 16:16).

3. **Knowledge**—Through the gift of the Holy Spirit (see 1 Corinthians 12:8) we are able to:

    - see things in the spirit, not seen in the flesh (see Jeremiah 11:18);

    - abound in knowledge as well as abound in the grace of God (see 2 Corinthians 8:7);

    - show our knowledge by our good conduct and conversation (see James 3:13).

4. **Revelation**—Through the gift of the Holy Spirit (see Ephesians 1:17) we are able to:

    - bring a profitable word to those around us (see 1 Corinthians 14:6);

    - receive understanding beyond the natural (see Galatians 1:12).

So let's review. You recognize that a conversation is heading toward an ungodly discussion. You follow the suggested approaches found in previous chapters, such as asking questions in an attempt to understand the motivation of the speakers: "Is this information that needs to be shared with me?" "Have you talked directly with the people involved in this scenario?" So what happens after you have questioned the person and made it clear that you are not interested in being a part of the evil report, but he or she persists in telling you? At this point, I encourage you to take a stand.

This may seem harsh or strong to some people, but *the magnitude of the consequences for not taking a stand far exceeds any discomfort or concerns about hurting the speaker's feelings.* Ephesians explains clearly what our response should be when confronted with "foolish talking" or "course jesting" (5:4). Let me share a few verses from Ephesians 5:

> For you were once darkness, but now you are light in the Lord. Walk as children of light (for the fruit of the Spirit is in all goodness, righteousness, and truth), finding out what is acceptable to the Lord. And have no fellowship with the unfruitful works of darkness, but rather expose them. For it is shameful even to speak of those things which are done by them in secret.
>
> verses 8–12

Another reference as to how we should respond to the carriers of evil reports is found in Romans 16:17: "Now I urge you, brethren, note those who cause divisions and offenses, contrary to the doctrine which you learned, and avoid them." I do not want to belabor the point, but I do desire for us to see the importance God has placed on dealing with people in our midst who create strife and division and speak evil of others.

═══ EXAMINING THE HEART ═══

1. Have you been contaminated within this past week?
2. Is there anyone you can think of who regularly contaminates you with his or her speech patterns? How can you now respond to this person?
3. Can you think of a time when you took a stand and refused to be a part of the contaminating conversation?

7

Subtle Seductions
in Conversation

Confusion and contamination, the subjects of the previous two chapters, are like twin locomotives powering us through the early stages of an uncontrolled conversation. By the time we reach the third stage, the whole process is gaining momentum. This stage is called foolishness.

Foolishness: Allowing an evil report to influence one's thinking and discernment about people and situations.

As a conversation unfolds into an evil report, the ensuing emotions can actually lead us to take up an offense against the person being criticized. Confusion and contamination have softened our defenses, and we fall into the trap of being sympathetic to the charges and not to the person. Our lack of discernment and wisdom can lead us to believe the accusations without ever checking out the facts or hearing, as Paul Harvey said, the rest of the story. Our foolishness affects our beliefs and behavior, and we become polluted with critical and negative thoughts.

Many people over the years have asked me to help them identify these carriers of evil reports, and I have come to focus on seven types or examples. The Bible speaks about each of these people, their character and the impact of their actions. This is not an attempt to categorize people or create our own misguided sense of righteous condemnation. Remember how easily our own thinking and discernment are affected! This list is not exhaustive and is to be used only as a guideline for further revelation from God. The examples are intended to help identify an evil report quickly so that we might avoid being defiled by ungodly conversation.

Seven Types of Evil Reporters

1. The Backbiter: one who speaks against an absent individual

The backbiter, to be sure, does not follow the Matthew 18 principle of reconciliation (discussed in a later chapter). All criticisms and comments, as the name implies, are made without the accused being present or behind his back. Psalm 15:2–3 speaks of this type of individual. Here David asks God who may dwell in His presence:

> He who walks uprightly, and works righteousness, and speaks the truth in his heart; he who does not backbite with his tongue, nor does evil to his neighbor, nor does he take up a reproach against his friend.

The word used for *backbiters* in Romans 1:30 is the word *katalalos* (*Strong's Exhaustive Concordance* #2637), which means "talkative against." Let me quote Romans 1:28–30 so you may get the full impact of this word:

> And even as they did not like to retain God in their knowledge, God gave them over to a debased mind, to do those things which are not fitting; being filled with all unrighteousness, sexual immorality, wickedness, covetousness, maliciousness, full of envy, murder, strife, deceit, evil-mindedness; they are whisperers, backbiters, haters of God, violent, proud, boasters, inventors of evil things, disobedient to parents.

The Bible places backbiters in the same company as the haters of God. Clearly God's people are to avoid these situations (see also Proverbs 25:23; 2 Corinthians 12:20).

2. The Busybody: one who seeks out information on a false report and spreads it by means of gossip, slander, backbiting, etc.

God takes this very seriously. In fact, He equates being a busybody with being an evildoer or even a killer. Some of you think this is mere sensationalism or exaggeration, but it is true; I have it on good authority. Look at 1 Peter 4:15: "But let none of you suffer as a murderer, a thief, an evildoer, or as a busybody in other people's matters." The idea of a busybody is also found in 1 Timothy 5:13: "And besides they learn to be idle, wandering about from house to house, and not only idle but also gossips and busybodies, saying things which they ought not." The Greek word for *busybodies* is *periergos* (*Strong's* #4021) and can be interpreted as "curious arts." In the neuter plural form of this word, the definition is "magic." This suggests that a person can weave a spell over another person by being a busybody. While we often think of a female as being a busybody, the Bible does not differentiate by sex. A male as well as a female can fall into this trap and become a tool of pain and suffering (see also 2 Thessalonians 3:11).

3. The Complainer: one who finds fault

This type of person often uses a personal situation as a platform for his or her complaint. "I was treated unfairly." "Do you know what this person did?" "You think that's bad, let me tell you what happened to me." Because the complainer shares from a personal perspective, the story embraces the emotions and creates an atmosphere of sympathy for the speaker's cause. Then we rush headlong down the track of foolishness, our willingness to listen leading us to a greater opportunity to be defiled and contaminated by this person. We must untangle our emotional connections to the complainer and recognize the violation of our spirits by the complaining individual. "Now when the people complained, it displeased the LORD; for the LORD heard it, and His anger was aroused" (Numbers 11:1). God will neither condone nor bless the complaining spirit. The complainer's motivation is to gain an advantage, be it spiritual, emotional or mental. Be aware of this subtle (and not so subtle) way of drawing you in (see also Jude 16).

This person is generally unhappy and wants to "share the wealth," so to speak. He or she is not fun to be around, and we often feel discouraged or depressed after being around this person. Hold up a mirror and evaluate your own attitude and actions. Do you look like you have been sucking on lemons? If I was having a rough day, are you someone I would want to be around to lift my spirit?

4. The Murmurer: one who grumbles

We find that this person is usually complaining but only loud enough for those in *close* proximity to hear. In fact, it may be so soft that a nearby person inadvertently asks him to repeat the offensive comment. The murmuring person is seldom happy or pleased with the outcome of situations. Like the complainer, he looks for faults and then justifies a bad attitude with his comments. Consistent with His focus, God speaks clearly to this type of behavior: "Do all things without murmurings and disputings" (Philippians 2:14 KJV).

One of the clearest examples in Scripture of grumbling and murmuring is found in Numbers 16. This is the story of Korah and his rebellion against Moses. How did Korah get hundreds of people to agree with him that Moses was simply exalting himself over the other Israelites? The Bible tells us that these were not just people of the congregation, but they were "leaders . . . men of renown" (verse 2). Can you see it happening? Perhaps Korah was jealous of Moses and Aaron. Perhaps Korah wanted more authority, recognition or power. Regardless of his motives, his methods are easily discerned. "Moses never treats us fairly." A person walking by might say, "What was that, Korah?" A few more comments about Moses thinking he was better than everyone, and people began to see Moses in a different way. How quickly they forgot the rescue out of Egypt, the parting of the Red Sea, the cloud by day and fire by night, manna from heaven, and quail provided as food.

Once we identify these people, their methods and their intent, their ways become clear to us. Korah simply went about poisoning the people and contaminating as many leaders *as would listen to him.* The end result was death to all those who opposed the positions that God had given to Moses and Aaron and, therefore, opposed God. How grateful and relieved the people must have been who said, "Korah, you are murmuring and I will not be a party to that type of conversation"—especially after Korah and his group were destroyed! They were as relieved as you will be after you face an encounter with a murmurer and turn from his foolishness (see also Jude 16).

5. The Slanderer: an individual who tries to injure someone's reputation or character by false and defamatory statements

"And the men, which Moses sent to search the land, who returned, and made all the congregation to murmur against him, by bringing up a slander upon the land" (Numbers 14:36 KJV). The word used in this Scripture for *slander* is the Hebrew word *dibbah* (*Strong's* #1681), which specifically means "evil report." Jeremiah speaks of those who slander in referring to the neighboring lands: "They are all stubborn rebels, walking as slanderers" (Jeremiah 6:28). This particular word means "scandal monger." An individual who slanders people is scandalous in God's eyes. This type of person may want to destroy or defame a reputation in order to be elevated in business, recognition or honor. The slanderer cannot be trusted to give accurate information, as his or her sole purpose appears to be self-serving. It is easy to see how slanderers defile and contaminate those who listen to their speech. It is for this reason that Paul includes them in his admonition about the qualifications of a deacon: "Likewise, their wives must be reverent, not slanderers, temperate, faithful in all things" (1 Timothy 3:11). Solomon, the wisest man in the land, wrote about the slanderer in Proverbs 10:18. He did not mince words: "Whoever hides hatred has lying lips, and whoever spreads slander is a fool" (see also Psalm 101:5; Jeremiah 9:4).

6. The Talebearer (or Gossip): a person who elaborates and exaggerates so as to make a story more dramatic (or "juicy")

"A talebearer revealeth secrets; but he that is of a faithful spirit concealeth the matter" (Proverbs 11:13 KJV). Just as God speaks seriously about the consequences and repercussions for those involved in an evil report, so He gives us specific guidelines to follow in our lives so as to avoid the pitfalls of the above behavior. Leviticus 19:16, in speaking about the covenantal laws of morality, states: "You shall not go about as a talebearer among your people; nor shall you take a stand against the life of your neighbor: I am the LORD."

If we associate with gossips and talebearers, we will become loose with our own tongues. The willingness to "discuss" other people becomes more a matter of habit than conscious choice. The more we are exposed to this, the more we contaminate our spirits. The Hebrew word for *gossip* and *talebearer* is closely associated with the word used for a *whisperer* (see number 7 below). (See also Proverbs 18:8; 20:19; 26:20, 22; 1 Timothy 5:13.)

7. The Whisperer: an individual who talks about other people privately, secretly and covertly in order to hurt them

Most of us have experienced the pain of association with the whisperer. This person uses the soft, hushed voice of secrecy to plot another's demise. Proverbs 16:28 states, "A perverse man sows strife, and a whisperer separates the best of friends." A whisper seems so innocent, so casual, even innocuous, yet it can destroy a person as it spreads like wildfire. One use of the word *whisperer* can be found in Psalm 41:7 when David writes, "All who hate me whisper together against me; against me they devise [plot] my hurt." The Hebrew word *lachash* is used in this context for *whisperer.* It means to "mumble a spell (as a magician)—a charmer" (*Strong's* #3907).

Not long ago I had dinner at a Chinese restaurant. At the end of the meal I opened my fortune cookie and read the inscription on the paper inside: "Speak only well of people and you need never whisper." While I do not put any merit in the *fortune* part of the cookie, I do think the person who wrote this particular statement was very wise.

The Pitfalls of Foolishness

Notice how many of the words from the previous seven examples are linked together by their Greek or Hebrew roots. Take note in particular of the words that are connected to the idea of spells or magic—manipulation, curses, subtle innuendos and accusations. We must avoid the pitfalls the enemy has placed before us. These pitfalls may not be adultery, gambling, alcohol, drugs, pornography or divorce—they are simply the words spoken by those around us; however, they are potentially every bit as dangerous and deadly as any other pitfall that may be placed in our paths.

It is imperative for us to remember how susceptible we are in the midst of a runaway conversation. *We are not always innocent lambs being attacked by the big "evil report" wolf.* I remember a few years back when I was the one doing the defiling.

It was a time when I was involved in coaching in the school system. One of the teacher/coaches I worked with was lacking in some areas of responsibility, which made working with him rather tiresome. It was well-known among the staff (and even the district) that Jim had an anger problem and was not the most responsible or organized individual. During the course of one week as I was talking with a supervisor about my coaching experience, we began to talk about Jim and, in a joking manner, went through a few of his escapades in the past months and years. As we continued, I began to recount some of my most recent frustrations with Jim, and the supervisor, likewise, shared his frustrations.

Later that evening, as I mulled over my part of the conversation, I realized that I had polluted the supervisor due to my speaking negatively about Jim. Now, everything I said was true. He was usually late for practice; he was disorganized; he left early; and he did lack certain people skills. However, it was not my place, nor my responsibility, to systematically address each of his shortcomings with the clear intent to injure his reputation. Again, I am called to be a light, to speak with a spirit of truth and humility.

Yet as I examined my motivation and my heart, I realized there was some malice and frustration in my conversation. I had defiled the supervisor and defrauded Jim. I was a whisperer, a complainer and a slanderer. Worse, I had failed to be a witness of Christianity in the midst of a secular system.

The next day I contacted the supervisor. I asked for his forgiveness for saying negative things about Jim. His response was one of shock and confusion. You see, in his eyes we did nothing wrong; we were part of a social setting in which cutting one another down and picking each other apart like vultures was fairly commonplace. He told me there was no need to say I was sorry, but I knew better. I explained that my speaking was not Christlike and did not create a positive environment—nor did it help Jim. After further discussion and testimony, the supervisor thanked me for my willingness to "take a stand." My honesty and intentions to create a godly atmosphere in the workplace were well received. I also developed a new prayer burden for Jim.

This incident took place many years ago, yet I will never forget it. I saw myself in a way that embarrassed me and that, I know, must have grieved the Holy Spirit. Sadly, this was not the last time I caught myself in this type of scenario, but the times of my defiling others are diminishing. I recently saw Jim, and the above incident was brought back to my memory. Gratefully, I am increasing in my self-control and not allowing the devil to use me as a tool of his torture.

We must properly prepare our spirits and minds to protect ourselves from these traps. In the same way that touching something diseased will defile one's hand, listening to an evil report will defile one's mind. Look at these additional Scriptures:

> You shall not circulate a false report. Do not put your hand with the wicked to be an unrighteous witness.
>
> Exodus 23:1

> And the men, which Moses sent to search the land, who returned, and made all the congregation to murmur against him, by bringing up a slander upon the land, even those men that did bring up the evil report upon the land, died by the plague before the LORD.
>
> Numbers 14:36–37 KJV

Obviously, this last Scripture uses several of the key words and examples that we have previously discussed. Even the people who did not bring the evil report, but merely listened and did not speak out against it, were killed.

The third track of defilement, foolishness, occurs when we are exposed to the negative aspects and attitudes of others, become confused and contaminated in our spirits and enter into *foolish practices and responses.* The Bible reveals this pattern over and over again and, notably, refers to the lives of all people—those who are believers in God and those who are not.

The Cyclical Pattern of Foolishness

The subtle seduction of an individual's life is indeed a tragedy, and unless we study and learn from it, this pattern will continue among the people of God. Remember, God loves all people and desires to have each one of us drawn toward Him.

In Exodus we have a prime example in Aaron and his tendency to become confused and contaminated and to move into areas of foolishness. Aaron had seen firsthand the faithfulness and power of God. He was able to partake in God's miracles and be a testimony to the certainty of the Word of God. Despite the constant haranguing of Pharaoh, Aaron was able to support Moses steadfastly in the deliverance of the Hebrew people.

Unfortunately, once the people were out of Egypt, doubt began to creep into their spirits and things began to change.

> And when Pharaoh drew near, the children of Israel lifted their eyes, and behold, the Egyptians marched after them. So they were very afraid, and the children of Israel cried out to the LORD. Then they said to Moses, "Because there were no graves in Egypt, have you taken us away to die in the wilderness? Why have you so dealt with us, to bring us up out of Egypt? Is this not the word that we told you in Egypt, saying, 'Let us alone that we may serve the Egyptians'? For it would have been better for us to serve the Egyptians than that we should die in the wilderness."
>
> Exodus 14:10–12

Aaron heard the complaints of the people. Was he also fearful? I believe some aspect of this negativity lingered in Aaron, planting a seed of confusion that would come to fruition.

It was not long before the children of Israel again began to murmur.

> Then the whole congregation of the children of Israel complained against Moses and Aaron in the wilderness. And the children of Israel said to them, "Oh, that we had died by the hand of the LORD in the land of Egypt, when we sat by the pots of meat and when we ate bread to the full! For you have brought us out into this wilderness to kill this whole assembly with hunger."
>
> Exodus 16:2–3

Did this murmuring and whining affect Aaron? Certainly he loved God and was strengthened by the miracles constantly unfolding in front of him. When the manna continued to bless the people for forty years, for example, should this not have quieted the complaints of the people and shown Aaron that negative reports and comments carried no validity in the sight of God? Somewhere along the line these words of doubt, complaining and murmuring had an impact on Aaron. He became confused and contaminated and, eventually, allowed the pressures from the people to move him into the level of foolishness. When did this happen, you might be thinking? Two words will remind you: golden calf!

The situation with the golden calf shows us Aaron's susceptible spirit. Remember what took place? Moses was on Mount Sinai, in the midst of the glory of God, receiving the Ten Commandments. With Moses gone, the people became impatient. An interesting note here: When people become impatient, confusion often enters into the thinking process. They feel they must solve the problem and avoid God's timing and the direction of the Holy Spirit. The more Moses delayed in coming down, the more nervous the people became. Finally they decided they wanted an idol built so they could worship. Aaron relented, gathered up the gold and made the idol of the calf. The gold they had was all from Egypt. They had been slaves there and had no possessions other than the gifts of gold, silver and clothing the Egyptians gave them upon their departure (see Exodus 12:35–36). The people of Israel were using the treasures of Egypt to erect an idol like the ones that the Egyptians had worshipped.

Moses came down from Mount Sinai and saw the people dancing and praying to the calf.

> And Moses said to Aaron, "What did this people do to you that you have brought so great a sin upon them?" So Aaron

said, "Do not let the anger of my lord become hot. You know the people, that they are set on evil. For they said to me, 'Make us gods that shall go before us; as for this Moses, the man who brought us out of the land of Egypt, we do not know what has become of him.'"

Exodus 32:21–23

Notice that Moses asked, "What did the people do to you?" He recognized that Aaron had been defiled by the interactions with the people, and with the usual defensiveness of a guilty person, Aaron responded by blaming the people and their evil nature. The first words out of Aaron's mouth should have been, "God, will You forgive me? And, Moses, will you forgive me?" Aaron had become contaminated by the previous interactions, and when confronted by the negative reports in Moses' absence, he was unable to endure their caustic nature.

This is how the level of foolishness occurs. We allow previous experiences to influence us: "Sandy has been having a rough time, and last week she was mad at me. So this time I won't confront her; I'll go along with her. What she said wasn't very nice, but it doesn't happen too often. I'll just love her." Loving her means *not* going along with her. Most incidents involving evil reports will likely be repeated unless there is intervention.

It would be nice if Aaron could be a testimony and an example of one who learned his lesson. It would be wonderful to say that Aaron was never confused or contaminated again, that in the future he did not endure foolishness and made wise decisions. Unfortunately, as it so often occurs in our lives, it takes multiple encounters with pain and sin to truly teach us that when you play with fire, it is easy to get burned. Let's look briefly at one other episode in Aaron's life.

There were many times when the people complained to Moses (and Aaron). In Numbers 11 we find a time when God was so displeased with the complaining that He created fire to consume some of the people in the outskirts of the camp. Once again, this murmuring and complaining created a questionable spirit within Aaron. We find this statement in the next chapter of Numbers:

> Then Miriam and Aaron spoke against Moses because of the Ethiopian woman whom he had married; for he had married an Ethiopian woman. So they said, "Has the LORD indeed spoken only through Moses? Has He not spoken through us also?" And the LORD heard it. (Now the man Moses was very humble, more than all men who were on the face of the earth.)
>
> Numbers 12:1–3

In verse 1, the word *spoke* means "to subdue or to destroy." Aaron was making an evil report against Moses. Having been affected by the congregation of Israel, he now took up his own offense and defiled others. This is the pattern of evil reports—cyclical. In my foolishness, I share something of an evil nature and you become contaminated. In your foolishness, you share a negative report and someone else gets contaminated. This repeats itself until the enemy has sufficiently divided a place of business, a family, friends and the Body of Christ.

As happened to Aaron, people who are involved in defiling others often seek to glorify self and flesh. This self-serving focus is a constant stumbling block to fellowship with God, as we see throughout history. Look at Cain, Jacob, King Saul, Absalom, Samson, Martha and Judas. Of course, the names could be more contemporary. The list could read: Mike, Tom, Sarah, Mary, Jim, Carol, Sandy, Brian . . . Our attempts to elevate self at the expense of others only lead to foolishness and prevent us from growing in our relationship with Christ.

It is essential that we are wise concerning the strategies of those who would draw us in by evil reports. Will your life be memorialized by a monument you built with negative words or by the godly character and actions of your life—prayer, servant-hood, grace, mercy, compassion, godly standards and uncom-promising integrity? Take a moment and ask God if you have any self-made monuments that have been erected in the name of foolishness and need to be destroyed. Repentance and willing-ness to submit to Christ will bring about purification in our lives.

EXAMINING THE HEART

1. What legacy or memorial are you leaving behind? Make a list of those qualities of God you wish to have displayed in your life.

2. Are there people around you who have created a subtle influence on you? Like Aaron, have you found yourself doing or saying "foolish" things that lead to areas of destruction?

8

Avoiding
False Alignments

Have you ever been chatting with someone, and as the conversation progressed, one of you commented, "We really have a lot in common"? The talk may have focused on jobs, interests, family, personal likes or dislikes. Regardless, something struck a cord of agreement between the two of you. This may signify the beginning of a new friendship or relationship. There seems to be something within us that is looking for agreement in others. It may be due to our own insecurities, our need for affirmation, a need for encouragement or even a vote of confidence.

The next time you are in a meeting, take note of the nonverbal approach of the speaker. His or her tendency will be to scan the audience for a listening ear. Once this has been established, the speaker will oftentimes lock in on that person, as if he or she were the only one in the room. Try this yourself. Maintain strong eye contact with the speaker (no staring with laser eyes!), nod your head in support and agreement, even smile when appropriate. You will find the speaker zeroing in on you more often. He has found an ally, someone to affirm him.

Now, I am not sharing this with you so we can do experiments on people in group settings, as if they were laboratory rats! Rather, I want to help you realize the power of agreement and the need within us for identification. We relate to those who affirm us. We draw strength from one another and utilize the agreement between us as a way to affirm our positions and attitudes.

Some years ago I was speaking to a group of professional people on the subject of teenagers. This was a secular setting, so the ideas and opinions offered from the audience regarding acceptable behavior, while diversified, leaned definitely toward a liberal viewpoint. When the subject of sexual behavior and promiscuity arose, several people spoke in support of health clinics in the public schools that offer contraceptives to students. After several minutes of general discussion, one of the participants asked for my opinion.

I hesitated for a moment as I surveyed the crowd. It was apparent this subject was one with a strong emotional base. After a moment or two, I ventured forth with my answer. "I find it rather curious and even disconcerting," I said, "that we, as a society, hand out condoms, birth control pills and needles to people and tell them to act responsibly when we have never taken the time to teach these same people how to be responsible." The array of facial expressions included glares, stares and grimaces. I continued, "We allow abortions without parental approval yet do little to facilitate parent-child communication. Children are told to be involved in 'safe sex' and not to drink and drive, but our societal framework teaches promiscuity and self-absorption—'If it feels good, do it. You are only accountable to yourself.'"

The more I talked, the more the majority of listeners expressed, shall we say, nonagreement in their facial and body languages. I continued to share from my heart and began searching the crowd for a friendly face, a nod of support, eye contact without the daggers. Now, I am not shy about speaking before groups, but I think that before long I must have attained that deer-in-the-headlights look. I wanted what every speaker hopes for—a reassuring look or smile of affirmation. I was looking for identification, someone in alignment with my belief system. While I learned later that many had agreed with me inwardly, I realized from this experience how strongly our human nature desires identification and alignment.

This type of connection has tremendous ramifications when related to evil reports. In the first place, most speakers desire alignment with their listeners, but it is a powerful driving force for those who give evil reports. In the second place, this same dynamic of identification affects those of us who listen to them. When we place ourselves in the position of hearing a negative conversation, our flesh seeks for identification as well. While I may not consciously want to agree, my soul hangs on every word, searching the memory banks of my mind and emotions for similar experiences and feelings. *Yes, I know that type of hurt,* I find myself thinking and, perhaps, my lips vocalizing.

Identification, then, is a powerful bond between people. It becomes a fourth track of defilement—a bondage, if you will—when used to unite people around an evil report.

Identification: Emotionally, intellectually, physically or spiritually connecting with another individual.

Does this happen that often? Are we really pulled into discussions by our commonalities? The answer to these questions is unequivocally yes! Identification can be positive when we draw godly strength and guidance from another individual or desire to be empathetic. If we are not careful, however, we may end up being tantalized, spiritually pulverized and eventually demoralized by this seductive process. True, effective empathy suggests the ability to examine a situation from another's perspective without becoming emotionally, mentally or spiritually distorted by it. But so often what begins as an attempt at empathy quickly slips into sympathy and feeling sorry for an individual. We try to make people feel better by sharing our own stories and areas of identification. If we have taken part in the early stages of deception—confusion, contamination, foolishness—it will not be long before we are trapped in the conversation and unable to pull away. This is the subtlety of identification.

While this process of identification is subtle, the approach used to deliver an evil report along this track can vary in its outward intensity. On the one hand, the person giving an evil report might take the Sherman Tank or Bulldozer approach ("I will run over you with my words"). In this case the reporter's desire for alignment is hard to miss—and sometimes hard to resist. On the other hand, the one giving an evil report might use a more subtle, seductive approach. Like a sniper he comes out of nowhere, causes injury and slips away before being detected. This individual is equally determined in his or her quest for identification, but the approach is vastly different. Let's look at both types so that we might be aware of the tactics and be better able to bring the evil report to a halt.

The Sherman Tank/Bulldozer Approach

As I mentioned earlier, I grew up in Phoenix, Arizona, and was a teenager during the turbulent 1960s. Marches for freedom, protests and riots about the Vietnam War seemed to polarize our country, the opposing sides tearing at the very core of our

nation. Questions abounded. Parents and children were separated by ideology, and a great chasm existed between generations. Still, in the midst of all this turmoil, people had a need
for identification. Two factions began to emerge in relation to
political beliefs regarding Vietnam—the Hawks and the Doves.
The Hawks were aggressive, interested in *winning* the war, even
at extreme cost. Increased military action, including bombing
Vietnam, was a popular focus of this group. On the other side,
the Doves were passive, believing we should never have entered
Vietnam. The Doves believed that the war was wrong, that we
were not supposed to get involved in the problems of another
country if it meant that Americans would be killed. While this is
a rather sketchy and simplistic overview of the groups, it shows
the desire to find commonalities.

For more than ten years the debate raged. People were torn
in their allegiances. In my own home, one brother was fighting
in Vietnam as part of the Marine Corps and another brother
was wearing black armbands and protesting the war. As you can
imagine, family gatherings were very, very interesting. Accusations, criticism and attacks were rampant throughout homes,
neighborhoods, cities and the nation.

The teenage years for me were challenging enough without
the emotional and psychological factors of wondering if I would
be drafted. The pressure (and need) to identify with one of
the groups, Hawks or Doves, was great. Which group would a
person join? It was a discussion that dominated our classes in
history, English and even math, depending on the day's occurrences in Vietnam.

People were far from subtle in their beliefs. Evil and distorted
reports were a constant part of the battle of words taking place
during the Vietnam era. Many would lie, change the facts and
deliberately try to deceive in an effort to garner support for their
strong views. One of my teachers who sided with the Doves,

for instance, would tell gory and painful stories about how the Vietnamese people, especially the children, were suffering because of the military action. Another teacher who sided with the Hawks would relate how the servicemen and women were being tortured by ruthless Vietnamese civilians who were only a front for the Vietcong.

Today I am a little unclear as to what I would do differently in some areas. One thing I do know: I would not rely on the strong-arm reports of others to gain my identification. I would do more research, find out the truth for myself. It was too easy to rely on the information of so-called experts because of their tank-like strength and persistence. Avoid allowing the Tank/Bulldozer approach to force you into a corner. Step away, think through the issues, do some more investigating and certainly evaluate your own experiences and personal values when relating to others.

The Sniper/Covert Approach

We see, then, that the Bulldozer approach is powerfully effective for creating alignments. This does not mean, however, that an evil report is effective only as it hits someone over the head with intensity. The sniper operates in subtlety and can be just as effective on his target.

A classic example of this latter approach is found in 2 Samuel 15:1–6. This tells the story of Absalom, disgruntled son of King David, and his sniper-like skill in using evil reports to his advantage.

After this it happened that Absalom provided himself with chariots and horses, and fifty men to run before him. Now Absalom would rise early and stand beside the way to the gate. So it was, whenever anyone who had a lawsuit came to the king for a decision, that Absalom would call to him and say, "What city are you from?" And he would say, "Your servant is from such and such a tribe of Israel." Then Absalom would say to him, "Look, your case is good and right; but there is no deputy of the king to hear you." Moreover Absalom would say, "Oh, that I were made judge in the land, and everyone who has any suit or cause would come to me; then I would give him justice." And so it was, whenever anyone came near to bow down to him, that he would put out his hand and take him and kiss him. In this manner Absalom acted toward all Israel who came to the king for judgment. So Absalom stole the hearts of the men of Israel.

Absalom used a seemingly innocent evil report (now, there is an oxymoron) to turn the hearts and affections of almost an entire nation and lead it in revolt against his own father.

The report emphasized Absalom's "care and concern" for the hurting people, his "righteous desire" that justice be done and his "ability" to be a better administrator than King David. He contrasted his apparent style and compassion with the people against David and his harsh, insensitive approach. By using words and no swords, spears or soldiers, Absalom stole the hearts of the people.

While it may appear that Absalom was a power monger, desiring to usurp his father's authority for the sake of his own ego, the root lies in the fact that David was guilty of poor parenting decisions regarding his son. It caused bitterness and rejection in Absalom that eventually surfaced as anger and rebellion.

The heart-wrenching breach between David and his son is found in 2 Samuel 13 and 14. Absalom had a sister named Tamar. A series of events occurred and Tamar was raped by her half brother Amnon. David was angry, yet took no action against the violation of Tamar. The years passed and Absalom exacted revenge for his sister by having Amnon murdered. Out of fear of reprisal by his father, Absalom fled the area for several years. Even though Absalom returned to Jerusalem (see 2 Samuel 14), David did not embrace his son or show him love and affection. David did not reach out to him for two years. It was not until Joab went to King David, on behalf of Absalom, that David met with his son. Even then, it was hardly a meeting of reconciliation. David did not extend forgiveness, the forgiveness that would have healed a scared, broken young man. This created a wound in Absalom, and he wanted to seek revenge against his father for the hurt.

The events surrounding Absalom and David may seem extreme, but the results are very typical when people are wounded in life. One becomes hurt by another. There is no clear reconciliation, and bitterness begins to creep in. Yes, the injured parties say that they are okay, but the seed of rejection and hurt begins to grow. It soon monopolizes their outlook on life, the way they relate to family, friends and situations. Emotionally injured people seek out others to align (or identify) with them, and as a result each person they speak to may become poisoned and pick up an offense. Absalom was very effective at "sharing the wealth" of his bitterness with others. We can learn how to avoid this type of person by further examining his subtle approach as outlined in 2 Samuel 15:1–6.

"After this it happened that Absalom provided himself with chariots and horses, and fifty men to run before him." Quickly, Absalom found fifty others to identify with his plight. As we have seen, this search for identification is typical of those who use evil reports to discredit others. By surrounding himself with like-minded followers, Absalom felt justified and empowered to come against the king. It is important to be wary of people who use others to validate their displeasure with a situation, as they will often step back and allow their followers to become the scapegoats if problems arise. Note that Absalom placed those people as a safeguard between the king and him-self: They ran before him. Evil reporters will protect them-selves at the cost of another person's reputation, character or future.

"Now Absalom would rise early and stand beside the way to the gate. So it was, whenever anyone who had a lawsuit came to the king for a decision, that Absalom would call to him and say, 'What city are you from?' And he would say, 'Your servant is from such and such a tribe of Israel.'" Absalom was smart; he chose people who had a grievance, people who already had a complaint. In chapter 2 of this book, I discussed how a car-rier of an evil report will test your spirit for compatibility. We see this taking place in this passage. Absalom is attempting to connect with individuals so that he can then draw them along-side his own cause. His first attempts are to find some common ground. This is usually how the stage of identification gains in power—through common hurts and frustrations. Absalom is appearing as a friendly neighbor asking personal questions, "small talk," to gain the confidence of the people.

"Then Absalom would say to him, 'Look, your case is good and right; but there is no deputy of the king to hear you.'" A sniper will do his best to sympathize with your situation, even to the point of supporting your grievance. He will pick up your offense and aid in substantiating your frustrations. Naturally his hope is that you will identify and reciprocate by supporting *his* issues. This is clearly the case for Absalom. He is attempting to engage them with a sympathetic spirit. Please note: The people coming to the king were following the procedures of the land. If they had a grievance, they were to come to the king for a dispute resolution. Each person coming to the king, however, must have been upset, offended and frustrated with his situation. Those of us who are prone to being offended are "ripe" for the enemy to come and pick us off.

"Moreover Absalom would say, 'Oh, that I were made judge in the land, and everyone who has any suit or cause would come to me; then I would give him justice.'" This reminds me of the scene from *The Wizard of Oz* where the Cowardly Lion sings, "If I were the king of the forest . . ." Absalom suggested—wistful and appealing in his comments—that if he were the representative of the people, everything would be done fairly and correctly. At that point, fueled by a desire for justice, the people found it easy to succumb to Absalom and his evil reports. These people had not even seen the king to air their grievances, but by feeding their fears of not being heard and understood, Absalom was able to align their spirits with his spirit. Are we just looking for a sympathetic ear to agree with us, or are we asking for people to speak the truth to us? I can remember many times being angry with someone because he spoke the truth to me. How about you? We respond in odd ways when truth pierces a lie, when light shatters the darkness. The more that Absalom approached the frustrated people, the more they began to whisper, murmur and agree with his polluted, malcontent spirit. Without even realizing what was happening to them, the people of the land became defiled. Absalom was encouraged by the results and continued to touch, contaminate and defile those who came to see the king.

"And so it was, whenever anyone came near to bow down to him, that he would put out his hand and take him and kiss him." Absalom was seeking acceptance and recognition. This continued each day, and Absalom grew in authority in the eyes of the people. However, the authority was usurped from the rightful leader. While David had refused years before to take this authority from King Saul, even though he had ample cause and opportunity (see 1 Samuel 24, 26), David's own son was quick to receive this ungodly adoration. People who are involved with evil reports often have a skewed perspective in life and feel insecure. The antidote, in their minds and spirits, is carnal recognition. We call this pride and arrogance. Some years ago, during a time of personal introspection, God showed me that my pride and performance mentality were actually based in insecurity. Until I find my security in Christ, I will look for recognition from people, materialism, performance and other worldly ways. Of course, only repentance, deliverance and healing from God will truly bring redemption to our lives and those we relate to in life.

"In this manner Absalom acted toward all Israel who came to the king for judgment. So Absalom stole the hearts of the men of Israel." In the Contemporary English Version we find it written as follows: "That's how he treated everyone from Israel who brought a complaint to the king. Soon everyone in Israel liked Absalom better than they liked David." Absalom carried out a tragic takeover of the nation with the help of those who were brought into alignment with an evil report. The foundation of Absalom's authority was based on deceit, mistrust, anger and bitterness and was spiritually illegal. Absalom was not given the authority by God; he latched on to the authority of men. Second Samuel 18 tells us of the demise of Absalom and all he tried to hold on to in the natural. In the end, the only way Absalom could be memorialized was by his own hand:

> When Absalom was alive, he had set up a stone monument for himself in King's Valley. He explained, "I don't have any sons to keep my name alive." He called it Absalom's Monument, and that is the name it still has today.
>
> 2 Samuel 18:18 CEV

It is fitting that Absalom's only testimony of his life—a life built on self-exaltation and the approval of others—was a monument he built to himself.

Safeguarding against False Alignments

And what about us? The search for commonality can be a natural and healthy experience. Yet when we investigate our motives, do we find pride, selfishness and a need for recognition?

Take a moment and ask God to expose those areas that conflict with His servant desires for you. Are you prone to identifying with individuals solely on the basis of what you have heard? Can you see the potential for involvement in runaway conversations if this propensity goes unchecked?

Learn to avoid the trap of falling into emotional identification by getting information for yourself. Compare your feelings and thoughts with the Bible's guidelines. Look for corroboration or contradictions as you assess the situation. And, finally, give a little more weight to the perspective of those who have been faithful, trustworthy and proven people of integrity than the words of a stranger or "expert" who has no track record of honesty.

I know I am not alone in my tendency to want to align myself with others. There are many times when my confidence is shaken and I look for some common ground. The problem is that I do not always pray and ask for the Father's guidance, nor do I always seek out godly counsel. Becoming aware of the pitfalls of false alignments makes it easier to discern when someone is attempting to manipulate and control our thinking.

Let's make this our prayer:

Dear heavenly Father, please expose those areas of my life that are in contradiction to Your will for me. I release my own selfish desires for personal gain and recognition. It is You, and You alone, who can exalt us in pure ways. My ways are known to You, O Lord, and I ask for You to change my ways to Your ways. For Your ways are truly higher than my ways, just as Your thoughts are higher than my thoughts. Thank You for Your steadfast love and faithfulness. Amen.

===== EXAMINING THE HEART =====

1. Are there people you usually talk to regarding certain situations because you will receive support and agreement from them?

2. Is there someone who can sway you with his or her Sherman Tank approach? Can you begin to make changes in your responses to this person?

3. Is there an Absalom in your life? Are there people, or a person, whom you have become sympathetic toward and are following toward destruction?

9

What Happens
When Fear Talks?

In Germany, they came first for the Communists, and I didn't speak up because I wasn't a Communist. Then they came for the Jews, and I didn't speak up because I wasn't a Jew. Then they came for the trade unionists, and I didn't speak up because I wasn't a trade unionist. Then they came for the Catholics, and I didn't speak up because I was a Protestant. Then they came for me, and by that time, no one was left to speak.

Martin Niemoeller, 1892–1984

My 1828 Webster's Dictionary defines the word *fear* as a "painful emotion or passion excited by an expectation of evil. Fear is accompanied by a desire to avoid or ward off the expected evil. Fear is an uneasiness of mind, upon the thought of future evil likely to befall us."

In its milder forms, fear can initiate a rush of adrenaline and be stimulating or even exciting; it is the reason many people enjoy roller-coaster rides or a scary moment in a movie (neither of which are on my top-ten list). But if fear persists to the point of becoming unmanageable or operates in extreme measures, it creates a tension so great that people say and do things they might not normally do. It short-circuits our spiritual discernment and may cause us to respond with ineffective thoughts, logic and emotions. Fear is captivating and creates a cycle of confusion that may lead to a serious path of hurt, pain and destruction.

This powerful emotion greatly affects our responses. It has a large impact on our participation in runaway conversations and is our fifth track of defilement.

> **Fear:** Anxiety-producing emotions that lead one to be concerned about losing control. This is often brought about by unexpected or poorly handled situations.

The connection might not be readily apparent. It is easy to wonder, for instance, how an evil report about an individual can create a fear response in us. We will look at this and other aspects of the fear cycle, as well as learn how to break free. The spiral of defilement is like a whirlpool of water. It is fascinating to look at and somewhat hypnotic, but if you get caught up in the current, it is very difficult to get out. As you spin around and around in the whirlpool, all points of reference get blurred. The fear cycle is one that spins us around to such an extent that we cannot identify the beginning from the end. Innocent comments seem like cutting remarks. Simple conversations become distorted and convoluted.

I remember swimming in the ocean during my college days in San Diego. I loved the waves crashing against the shore, the taste of salt on my lips, the fresh smell of the sea. I spent many hours enjoying the sun, the surf and the sand. (Naturally, this was *after* I had finished going to class, doing my homework and studying for every test. Well, maybe it was before, or instead of, I can't remember—it is such a convenient blur!)

In any event, I specifically enjoyed bodysurfing in the ocean. I would swim out to where the waves began to grow on their way to cresting and then breaking. As the water would swell around me, I would swim along with it. The key was to be swimming in the wave as it crested. The momentum of the wave would then carry me toward the shore. When it was done properly, I could actually be propelled along in the midst of the wave with my head out of the water and enjoy a free water ride.

Occasionally, however, the wave would suddenly break on the shore and crash down with me in the middle of it. The turbulence of the water would spin me around, over and over again until I could not tell which way was up. I remember times when my lungs were ready to burst yet my body continued to be tossed to and fro underwater like a piece of seaweed. I would try frantically and desperately to swim toward the surface only to realize I was swimming sideways or, worse yet, toward the bottom. The feeling of panic and fear only magnified my confusion and my misdirection until finally I achieved freedom from the watery prison and could gulp big breaths of air.

Likewise, when we place ourselves in a position amenable to gossip and murmuring, the emotion of fear empowers the areas of confusion, contamination, foolishness and identification, all leading to defilement. The panic that comes with fear causes us to think that we must respond immediately with exceptional force and conviction. As in my ocean experiences, our perspective becomes distorted; we attempt to reach for "fresh air" only to realize we have gone in the wrong direction. This only reinforces the panicky emotions and elevates the desperate nature of our actions. If we continue to develop this pattern in our lives, each situation becomes more and more unclear as we react to people with confusion, judgment, criticism and condemnation. Further, it is the emotion of fear that opens the door for the dangerous stage of impurity, which will be discussed in the next chapter.

To Fear or Not to Fear

Certainly there are times when fear is good. Fear and anxiety can warn of imminent danger: A little child may be fearful to cross a busy street by herself; an adult may be fearful of walking alone in certain areas. These can be lifesaving motivations. It becomes important, then, to have an understanding of fear and the wisdom to know what to fear.

Here are some Scriptures to help us gain an appropriate perspective on fear.

- "The LORD said to me, 'Gather the people to Me, and I will let them hear My words, that they may learn to fear Me all the days they live on the earth'" (Deuteronomy 4:10).
- "Serve the LORD with fear, and rejoice with trembling" (Psalm 2:11).
- "The fear of the LORD is clean, enduring forever" (Psalm 19:9).
- "The fear of the LORD is the beginning of knowledge, but fools despise wisdom and instruction" (Proverbs 1:7).
- "Honor all people. Love the brotherhood. Fear God. Honor the king" (1 Peter 2:17).

While the admonition to fear God is clear, the Lord also gives the command *not* to fear.

- "'But do not fear, O My servant Jacob. . . . No one shall make him afraid'" (Jeremiah 46:27).
- "'Do not fear, O Jacob My servant,' says the LORD, 'for I am with you'" (Jeremiah 46:28).

Fear. . . . Do not fear. . . . It might sound paradoxical upon first glance. I believe the key is found in this verse: "In God (I will praise His word), in God I have put my trust; I will not fear. What can flesh do to me?" (Psalm 56:4). In other words, trust in God, not in man. Fear the Lord, flee from evil.

How are we fearful of God? By giving Him honor, respect and reverence for His power and authority. "The fear of the LORD is to hate evil; pride and arrogance and the evil way and the perverse mouth I hate" (Proverbs 8:13). God never intended fear to bring bondage to our lives. It is meant to guide us and keep us safe under His protective covering.

Unfortunately, in circumstances where false reports are being uttered, the fear of the Lord is usually overlooked. Our trust is placed in the constant barrage of negative and condescending remarks and inaccurate information. This takes a terrible toll on us as our defenses are gradually worn down. We begin to reject the truth we know, the people we love and the destiny to which God has called us. We begin to anticipate, fixate on negative outcomes—surely accidents, broken relationships, injuries, rejection and hurt are just around the corner. As stated earlier in this chapter, our responses become atypical of us (as godly men or women) and typical of a defiled person.

Faith does not operate in the realm of fear. In fact, it could be said that fear is the opposite of faith. Remember the definition of fear stated earlier: "an uneasiness of mind, upon the thought of future evil likely to befall us." We cannot dwell on God's goodness if our minds are full of fear.

It was during a recent time of ministry with a couple in our church that my wife, Joyce, and I saw the full effect of fear. The couple was struggling in their marriage and asked for counsel and prayer. Their problems were serious.

Even though the couple expressed little hope for their marriage, Joyce and I spoke words of faith and encouragement to them. We serve an awesome God whom we have seen take broken lives and marriages and restore them miraculously. At one point, when it appeared we were not making headway, Joyce pressed in a little deeper. "It seems you have made up your minds about your marriage. What kind of feedback have you had regarding the future of your marriage?" This question was asking the couple to divulge the source of input for their lives. Was it the Bible? Prayer? Godly counsel with friends? Ministry leaders? The next-door neighbor? A person at work? Someone who had gone through similar trials?

The next few minutes were very telling in the lives of this couple. They both had listened to friends who had been divorced or were separated. It became evident that the constant negative input had filled them with fear. They were confused and hurting. They both acknowledged the tendency to identify with the problems they heard and negate the possibility of solutions. "My wife (or husband) does that, too" was a common rejoinder for them in those conversations.

May I tell you the phrase that tipped us off? We have heard it many times, and whenever we hear it spoken, we know that the individuals have been polluted by the world's views. This phrase tells us that God is not a part of their thinking and that they have moved into a fear of the world, of life and of the future. The phrase is this: "I have given to others all my life and now I need to look out for myself." This is the same as saying, "I no longer want to serve. . . . I am more important than anyone. . . . Meeting someone else's needs is not as important as meeting my own needs." I will come back to this situation later in this chapter.

The Resurrection of Lazarus

Let us look at a biblical account involving Jesus and some very dear friends. Take note that constant negative and false reports had great impact on the thinking of people in biblical times, also, to the point that even those who knew Jesus well lost sight of who He really was and of His authority.

Mary and Martha and their brother, Lazarus, enjoyed a special relationship with Jesus. He had spent time at their house, both socializing and ministering. Mary is remembered as the one who anointed His feet with oil and wiped them with her hair (see John 12:3). The Bible says explicitly, "Now Jesus loved Martha and her sister and Lazarus" (John 11:5). It is very evident that Mary, Martha and Lazarus had spent time with Jesus.

During their times of "connecting" with one another and building relationships, of course, the air around them swirled constantly with charges and allegations about Jesus. The city of Bethany, the home of Mary, Martha and Lazarus, was an oppressed area. It was also known as the "house of misery" because of its reputation for welcoming many physically injured and emotionally hurting people. Certainly the people felt rejection and complained of their lot in life. How many times were curses made toward Jesus regarding the assertion of His being the Christ? Certainly the Pharisees belittled and besmirched His name. Is it possible that after such a barrage even Mary and Martha finally got worn down? Could fear have found its way into their hearts due to the persistent spirits of confusion and contamination that surrounded them daily?

In John 11 we follow the account. Lazarus was ill, and his sisters sent a message to Jesus that their brother was sick. Note, however, this critical point: The message was not "Lazarus is sick" but "Lord, behold, he whom You love is sick" (John 11:3). Jesus cared deeply for Lazarus. He was a friend; they had a personal relationship. My perception is that because of this connection there was an expectation that Jesus would hurry to be with the family. But Jesus did not go to see Lazarus immediately, and instead stayed where He was for two more days. Then He decided to go to Judea, a place where there was animosity against Him. I imagine there was much discussion among the disciples. "Why is He waiting to go to Lazarus?" "Judea? Is that a wise choice?" Even though Jesus (whose miracles were well-known and whose word was always true) revealed to the disciples that Lazarus had died but that He would "wake him," they found little to be encouraged about. Thomas made a most telling comment when they departed for Judea: "Then Thomas, who is called the Twin, said to his fellow disciples, 'Let us also go, that we may die with Him'" (John 11:16). Now, that is an encouraging send-off! I suppose the name "doubting Thomas" was appropriate for this reason.

When Jesus and His disciples finally reached Bethany, Lazarus' dead body had been in the tomb for four days. When word came that Jesus had arrived in town, Martha left the house, where many people had gathered to comfort her and Mary, to meet Him. Or rather, she was up and on the move ready to confront the Son of God. Is it surprising that Martha headed toward Jesus, wanting a discussion, while Mary sat still in the house? (See John 11:20.) Remember, it was Mary who sat at the feet of Jesus, listening contemplatively, while Martha was active, busying herself with work.

Martha immediately engaged Jesus in conversation. Her statement was respectful, showing a degree of former faith yet lacking in active faith. "Now Martha said to Jesus, 'Lord, if You had been here, my brother would not have died'" (John 11:21). Martha knew Jesus could have saved Lazarus. She had seen and heard of many of His miracles. It was for this reason they sent word to Jesus and asked for a healing for their brother.

Yet fear had robbed her of active faith—faith that can be called upon in the present. When all seems bleak, when there is no visual substance to believe, it is our active faith that wells up within us and awaits the touch from God. "Now faith is the substance of things hoped for, the evidence of things not seen" (Hebrews 11:1).

If Martha had not let fear swallow her faith, she would have asked God to speak forth words of life. Fear altered her perception. Martha's mind began to run away with her thoughts, and instead of being drawn toward God she was pulled away.

In response to her comments, Jesus spoke these words: "Your brother will rise again" (John 11:23). Martha's lack of faith was again blatantly obvious in her words. She did not acknowledge the possibility of a miracle, but instead noted that Lazarus would rise, like all dead people, in the day of resurrection.

Thus my impression is that Martha and Mary had been polluted by the words of those around them. Instead of having a clear vision about the possibilities in God, they were discouraged and walked in fear of the truth. They resigned themselves to the death of Lazarus, even though "the resurrection and the life" (John 11:25) stood in their midst. Did they not understand the healing power of Jesus? They had faith in the ability of God to heal their brother of sickness yet were unable to extend that faith to resurrection from death to life.

Is God to be so limited by us? When we begin to place limitations on the power of God, we enter into a "wilderness" mentality. Remember the Hebrew people and the countless miracles of God they witnessed. Plagues were sent upon the Egyptians to open up the opportunity for them to be free. The Red Sea parted so they could pass through, and then, as suddenly as it parted, it closed upon their enemies. And still the Israelites continually placed limitations upon God. "We don't have enough food; we are going to die." "We are thirsty; we are going to die." "We are surrounded by our enemies; we are going to die." They limited God in His authority and power in their lives.

How do people who know of God's divine power place barriers and restrictions upon Him? Mary and Martha were not able to seize upon their active faith because they had been polluted by discouragement and confusion. This blindness to the ability of Christ to heal their brother, to raise him from the dead, was mainly due to fear. But where did this "pollution and fear" come from?

The words spoken to Martha and Mary had indeed penetrated deeply. John 11:19 speaks of how people gathered around to "comfort" them. This is mentioned again in verse 31. Was godly solace for the bereaved really taking place? More likely the comforters gave in to the temptation to speak negative comments about Jesus and His "unwillingness" to come when He knew that His friends desperately wanted Him.

The Greek word used for *comfort* in John 11:19 and 11:31 is *paramutheomai* (*Strong's* #3888). It is derived from another word, *muthos* (*Strong's* #3454), which means "a tale, fiction, fable." Were the words being told to Mary and Martha by the friends around them a myth, a fable? Were they being ministered to by fairy tales? It appears the words spoken to Mary and Martha contained fabrications and exaggerations.

Their minds must have been racing, hearing every comment made by the unbelieving crowd. "See, I told you He wouldn't come." "He wasn't really your friend." "Why did He wait before coming here? He doesn't care about us." And then, when Jesus did arrive, Martha acted in a way contrary to her belief system. She made a negative confession, one that displayed the current condition of her heart . . . one struggling with faith. She had become confused, hurt, bewildered and fearful. The evil reports cloaked in soothing words had allowed deep fear and doubt to rise up in both Martha and Mary. No longer did they see Jesus as the healer, the Lord of life, but only as one who let them down.

In this story we have an excellent example of how to combat fear in the face of powerful runaway words. Jesus did not argue, debate or fight with Martha. He simply told her the truth. He reiterated the truth. "Your brother will rise again" (verse 23). "He who believes in Me, though he may die, he shall live" (verse 25). "And whoever lives and believes in Me shall never die" (verse 26). Jesus concluded by asking Martha a poignant question: "Do you believe this?" (verse 26). The direct, honest and loving way in which Jesus approached Martha brought clarity to her. She was able to see through the fear and realize the significance of what she had been saying. Martha told Jesus that she knew He was the Christ, the Son of the living God, who had come to the world (see John 11:27). Once the truth was recognized and confessed, the cloud of confusion and fear lifted. With the truth shining in her heart, Martha was able to bring her sister to Jesus.

However, notice in verses 28–32 that Martha secretly goes to Mary and then states that Jesus was asking for her. Why secretly? She now recognized the power of the negative reports and did not want to be assaulted by them again. Then, in order to avoid Mary arguing with her, she says that Jesus asked for her personally (which was not true). And then, with the same attitude and exact same verbiage, Mary says to Jesus, "If you had been here, my brother would not have died." How interesting that both Mary and Martha use the exact same statement in separate conversations. Do you think they might have heard this phrase (and many others) from their friends who were comforting them with myths and fables?

Jesus was overcome with compassion and love for Mary and Martha. He was not angry or upset, but returned their words with kindness and truth. And even as He wept over their pain, He brought triumphant life back to their midst with the raising of Lazarus. We, too, should speak with words of love, compassion and kindness to those trapped in fear.

This was a watershed event for those who surrounded Jesus. Like Martha and Mary many saw and believed, but many others chose to continue with poisonous words against Him: "But some of them [who had seen Lazarus walk out of the tomb] went away to the Pharisees and told them the things Jesus did" (verse 46). Fear of Roman reprisals because of Jesus' popularity drove the Pharisees to put their words into action: "Then, from that day on, they plotted to put Him to death" (verse 53).

Fear can draw us toward God or pull us away. It can create a desire in us to cling to the truth or alter our perception of the truth. While Satan wants to use fear to rob us of our faith in God, we need to continue to speak words of truth and confidence regarding our place with Christ.

A Personal Example

We saw in the example of Martha and Mary what can happen when words of truth crash through words of doubt and fear. These words came from Jesus Himself, but truth may also come from a friend, from the Bible or from any number of likely sources. However, it may also come from the very person who placed the fear in you, the source of the anxiety and defilement. Let me share a personal example.

Having made a change in my teaching status, I moved to a different building and was teaching at a different grade level. I was excited about this change and anxious for God to use me in this area. During the first few days all seemed promising: I met many of the teachers and was feeling very much a part of the staff. At the end of the first week, however, I had an encounter that influenced me for the rest of the year. One conversation, one quick dialogue and I became "trapped" for the next nine months. Fear is an odd emotion. It can come upon us so quickly, so suddenly. Before we even have a chance to respond, fear begins to wrap its tentacles around our hearts and minds.

I was walking down the hallway on my way to lunch and I passed by Karen. She was a teacher in her mid-thirties, whom I had met briefly in a meeting. I smiled at her and said, "Hello, Sharon." She looked at me, unsmiling, and corrected me regarding her name. I apologized sheepishly, attributing my mistake to being new and meeting so many people. Getting no response, I continued to chat casually, commenting about the number of students in the hallway and how crowded it was to walk. She received my efforts with a stern, steady scowl. My thirty-thousand-dollar education and my counseling credentials helped me discern immediately that something was amiss. Or, perhaps, it was the hole that was now bored in my head from her steely glare. Regardless, I knew we were not connecting very well and fear began to approach. I asked her if I had said something wrong. Her response helped fear get a tighter grip on my mind. "Why would you care?" she said. "It's not like you would change." She retreated into her classroom as the bell rang, signaling the beginning of the next period.

I gulped, took a deep breath (actually a shallow breath because I felt as though someone was choking me) and followed her into her classroom. I was not sure what to say, but I knew something needed to be done. I had no desire to go through the rest of the day or week with someone upset with me. "Karen, could we meet after school to talk? I'm sorry if I have offended you." There was a bit of pleading in my voice. Again a withdrawn, distant response came forth: "It would be a waste of time. Your arrogance would get in the way." With that she turned her back and the conversation was over.

Dejected and in shock, I walked down the hallway wondering how to respond. My mind was confused as I replayed the conversation over and over. What *had* I said? Was she right?

Right about what? It did not make any sense to me. And worse yet, there was no hiding from the problem: Her room was on the same floor as mine. I would be passing by her door several times a day. Was it too late to change jobs?

Within minutes another teacher tracked me down. She asked how I was doing. I suppose that having my lower lip drag on the floor gave a slight indication that something was not right. This teacher explained that she had been in the hallway and had heard the conversation. I shook my head and had few words to offer in reply. The teacher told me to not take it personally as Karen had done this to many other teachers, especially men. She had had several bad experiences in past relationships and was bitter. From the consoling teacher's perspective, Karen was an angry person who often responded to people with venom and rage. Over the next half hour, two other teachers approached me in an attempt to offer encouragement.

Yet as the school day ended, I could not shake the heaviness upon me. I went to the principal in an effort to obtain counsel. When I sat down in his office, he said, "Sounds like you met Karen today." I smiled weakly as I realized that the story had probably spread throughout the school (the joy of gossip!). I shared my perspective and asked if I should approach her again, apologize and attempt to smooth over the situation. His counsel was to leave it alone, as he concurred with the other staff members regarding her anger. He shared that she was a fine teacher, but she struggled with relationships with fellow staff members. I was told she was much "better" than she used to be with people. That was not much comfort.

As the weeks passed I found clever ways to avoid Karen. I walked to the other end of the hallway to get wherever I was going, even if it was just to the other side of her doorway. If she came into the office, I walked out. When she was walking toward me, I reversed direction or ducked into the nearest room. This may sound childish (because it was), but I was scared of another encounter with her. I felt handcuffed, unable to approach her to reconcile, yet bound by the curses she had leveled at me. I spent time in prayer, hoping to get a direction for working with her. It was the end of October when I felt an inspiration to reach out again.

The student government was selling candy-grams as a fundraiser. I purchased a little pumpkin-shaped card and wrote a note to Karen.

> *Dear Karen,*
>
> *I am sorry we got off on the wrong foot. If I have been insensitive, please forgive me. I hope you have a great day and I look forward to working with you this coming year.*
>
> *Sincerely,*
>
> *Mike Sedler*

The cards were given out on Halloween, but I did not receive any response. Throughout the year, there were numerous occasions where I found myself in the copy room, in the office or walking down the hallway and there was Karen. Occasionally, she would be cordial and say hello. Other times she would ignore me. Each time, my heart would begin to pound and I would look for an escape route. I never did reach out again to Karen. I was gripped by fear and was unwilling to place myself in a position of being hurt again with no known chance of reconciliation.

The last week of school arrived. It was early morning before classes and I was cleaning up my room for the upcoming summer break. I looked up and in my doorway was Karen. The windows were closed and locked; she was blocking the only doorway. I am sure the look on my face was one of terror. I got a grip on myself, straightened up my five-foot-six-inch frame, looked at her boldly (I am sure I was an impressive sight) and said, "Hi." She asked if I had a moment to talk. The grip of fear came upon me and all I could think about was the conversation nine months earlier. My confidence was gone; no Scriptures of encouragement came to mind. I had let fear literally rob me of my faith, hope and confidence in God.

I answered Karen in the affirmative and asked her to come into the room. Her words were cautious, but purposeful. Her voice had a tone of lightness mixed with a twinge of sadness. As I listened to her speak, the fear began to dissipate, being replaced with compassion and love for a wounded sister. "Mike, I'm sorry," she began slowly. "Earlier in the year, I should not have said the things I did to you." In my haste to make things better, I quickly interjected, "It's okay. I'm sorry if I was insensitive." She persisted, "No, it wasn't you. It is me. I have a lot of issues that need to be taken care of in my life. I am moving out of the area and taking another job. I shouldn't have taken my frustration out on you. I appreciate your reaching out to me. I am sorry I couldn't respond. Please forgive me." My smile and words of forgiveness seemed to lift a weight off her shoulders. She shook my hand, turned and walked away. As I stood watching her in disbelief, the Lord began to reveal my sin.

I had ridden along the track of fear to such an extent that it had prevented me from praying for a hurting individual. My own emotions had paralyzed me. Instead of recognizing the opportunity to pour out God's love, I became frightened and distant. Fear had thrown such a blanket of confusion upon me that I was unwilling, not unable, to persist in an area of outreach. I say "unwilling" because I know God's power and authority could easily have purged the fear from my thoughts if I had allowed Him. First John 4:4 says it beautifully: "You are of God, little children, and have overcome them, because He who is in you is greater than he who is in the world."

Fear infected my opportunity to minister, to reach out and perhaps even to evangelize another person. Karen should not have "attacked" me verbally, but it was my sin, the sin of holding on to fear, of looking out only for myself, that prevented her from being healed that year. The one who spoke fear into my life was also the one who opened my eyes to the truth of God. I am so grateful for Karen and her willingness to speak to me the last week of the school year. She not only freed me from my fear, but she was a vehicle for God's teaching me a valuable lesson.

I do not know where you are today, Karen, but if by some exciting design of God you are reading this book, I wish to write you one more note.

Dear Karen,

I am sorry I was not more sensitive to you and your situation. I know God has great love for you and a desire to see you healed of past hurts. I lift up a prayer for you and trust that God has brought others into your life to touch and heal your broken heart. May your life be full of joy.

Sincerely,

Mike Sedler

Speaking Truth

Earlier in this chapter I mentioned a counseling session Joyce and I had with a couple who had taken on the posture of negativity brought about by fear. Our approach to them was simple: We followed the approach that Jesus used with Martha. No, we did not tell them that we were the "resurrection and the life," but we did begin to speak truth to them. We discussed the words that had been spoken over them. We reminded them that they had a calling on their lives and recounted the ways in which God had used them to minister to others. We had them review their dreams. As they listened and then began to talk about shared areas of their lives, it was as if the veil or cloud was lifted from them. They began to weep and ask for forgiveness for their loss of hope. They spoke words of commitment to one another and words of healing.

This is not to say they had no more issues to deal with in their marriage. But they are together today, working through their problems via counseling, accountability, prayer and support.

If you are in a situation where fear has robbed you of hope and dreams, take a moment to ask for God's clarity in your life. Fear will try to negate the truth by overshadowing it with worry and false scenarios. *Speak truth to your fears.* Do it now! If your marriage seems too broken to be fixed, your relationship with your children too cold ever to connect again, stop now and pray. Write out the truths of your life, the areas of success, of relationships, of support and encouragement. Too often, our fear will lead us to a path where we only see the darkness and cannot see the light.

═══ EXAMINING THE HEART ═══

1. Do you remember a time when fear was gripping your decisions and your perspective? How did you handle it? Is it still a problem? If so, read the above prayer again.

2. Like Martha, do you ever have faith in God only to have it stripped away? What changes can you make to keep this from happening?

3. Make a list of areas in which you allow fear to come into your life. Share this list with a trusted friend and begin to pray against those open areas.

10

How to Judge Impurity

In this chapter, we will explore the impact an evil report has upon the listener. This brings us to the sixth track of the journey of those who embrace an evil report: impurity. While impurity is far from subtle in its entirety, it may work its way subtly into people's lives. One word here, a comment there, even a nonverbal gesture may hasten us on our way. Impurity can have a violent impact on the spirit. It creates false impressions and leads to the final destination of one who will not be swayed from evil reports: deception. Deception is the topic of the next chapter. Here is our working definition of impurity.

> **Impurity:** When one receives an evil report from a person, takes it into his or her spirit and, even though it is contrary to other information already known, refuses to explore further truths and believes it to be true.

Defilement on a Large Historical Scale

During the 1930s and 1940s a man by the name of Adolf Hitler used the spirit of impurity to defile an entire nation and pollute millions of other people. His approach was simple but diabolical. He mesmerized the people into believing that he had a plan, a direction that would lead them to a better life. This included pointing out those people (Jews, the elderly, the handicapped, homosexuals, gypsies) who would interfere with the plan and how they were creating a barrier to the future of Germany. It was a slow, appealing seduction. His oratorical skills, charismatic gestures and convincing concepts blinded morals and reshaped truth. Impurity, while violent in its nature, is very crafty in implementation. Initially Hitler was not popular among the people. He was seen as emotionally unstable and extreme in his ideology and his approach. But the people continued to listen even though they may not have agreed. In time confusion set in, then contamination and each track of defilement pulled the listening populace deeper into impurity. Slowly, cleverly and artfully, Hitler polluted a nation with impure words and deeds.

As we saw earlier in our study of David's bitter son, Absalom, Hitler surrounded himself with others who had similar beliefs and convictions. There were many who were unsure what they believed so they followed the group, the crowd. The Nuremberg war trials brought legal conviction to many of the guards and officers in the concentration death camps for their part in the killing of millions of people. The most common defense of these soldiers was "I was just following orders." To many of us, this grotesque and hideous occurrence is inconceivable. How could anyone be a part of these atrocities? Had they no conscience? Where was their sense of morality? For some, I can tell you the answer. Impurity had blinded them to common sense. All of their understanding was poisoned, desecrated. Individual thought had given way to group priority. And the group priority was directed by a man who was bitter and polluted with hatred and self-exaltation.

I grew up in a Jewish home. I had my bar mitzvah at the age of thirteen and went through my confirmation classes at the age of sixteen. The majority of my friends were Jewish and the bulk of my social life involved Jewish activities. I was part of a youth group that met at the Jewish Community Center and regularly attended the functions. We had citywide gatherings, dances and sporting events. Each year we had a statewide youth event in Arizona with special speakers and an inspirational focus. All this was geared toward encouraging our Jewish faith and way of life.

I remember one such weekend when a rabbi from another city shared about prejudice and hatred toward the Jewish people. In giving us a historical perspective of the persecution of Jews, he emphasized the lies that were spread in early history and how they increased during the years of the Roman Empire. He spoke of the deception of Gentiles (non-Jews) and how their hatred for the Jews infiltrated the cultures of the world. The Jewish people were blamed for the death of Christ, and this bias led to the death of many Jews over the past two thousand years.

At the end of that weekend gathering, I realized that being Jewish could separate me from others in my life. In fact, I grew aware of an apparent ominous and general disdain for Jewish people from certain prejudiced and narrow-minded individuals. Suddenly each conversation that carried any hint of anti-Semitism was magnified in my life. I realized that comments like "I jewed him down," which meant, "I talked him down to a lower price," were rampant in my predominantly non-Jewish school. I listened to disparaging remarks that non-Jews made about financial success or educational accomplishments in Jewish families. The ignorance of those who used these expressions only solidified my growing segregation from non-Jews.

It was during this same year that my awareness exploded into reality through two powerful visual events. The first was a fight at my school that started when a boy called a friend of mine "a dirty Jew." The other comments I had heard at school were painful, but this was the first time that I felt prejudice actually directed toward me, a personal attack on my culture and religion. After this the racism projected toward people of color or varying cultures also became more vivid to me.

The second event came not much later: Our history teacher hung a Nazi flag in his room as we studied Germany and World War II. This brazen act was disturbing to those of us who were Jewish, and others were uncomfortable with it as well. To study the historical facts of a war was one thing, but to display the flag of an army that killed six million people of my own heritage was a terrible insult. One young girl in my school burst into tears as she recalled the story of her grandparents being killed in the "showers without water" by the Nazi regime. It seemed the more I looked, the more I saw. A few years later, during the 1972 Olympics, when Israeli athletes were killed for being Jewish, my concern and confusion only deepened.

When I went to college, this confusion was amplified. I left Phoenix and went to a school in San Diego. I was surrounded by strangers and without my support systems. My loving parents were not around, nor were my high school friends. Again, the prejudice was blatant. I kept my religious beliefs to myself for the first months, cautious as to the response from my fellow classmates. As time progressed, however, I began to explore the attitudes of those around me. My personal confidence and pride in being Jewish allowed me to be more assertive. "Why would you call a Jewish person a cheapskate?" I asked. "What do you mean, you jewed him down?" I challenged. In time, it was apparent to me that most people had no idea what they were talking about. They had been raised in homes that spoke these phrases, which had become a part of their own vocabulary. The impurity that surrounded them had shaped their own personal viewpoints. I began to see some of these people with a new understanding, almost pity. They had allowed a polluted and foolish spirit to manipulate their perspectives.

Yet as I look back upon my own life, I see how this was true for me, also. I considered Germans en masse as killers and murderers. It was unfathomable to me that anyone could allow the deaths of so many Jewish people without raising a hand. You see, I had never heard of Corrie ten Boom, Dietrich Bonhoeffer, Oskar Schindler or the countless others who had stood for godliness during this heinous time. In fact, I did not know that millions of Christians had also died in that Holocaust. Like those around me, I had allowed my own inward perception to create a fog-like mentality toward the truth about others.

Impurity clouds our perspectives. We begin to see and hear those who appear confident, sure and right. Those raising dissenting voices are viewed as weaklings, shortsighted. Our own convictions are put on the shelf as we get caught up in the charisma of the moment. The synergy of emotions can overwhelm us to such an extent that we begin to question our own beliefs and attitudes. This is not necessarily bad if we pursue truth and honesty and engage in a mission to strengthen personal belief systems. It was through one of these times of searching for truth and the challenges to my own perspectives that allowed me to hear of the reality of Jesus Christ.

When I was 22 years old, God revealed the truth of Christ's dying for my sins and His resurrection life. For more than 35 years I have walked in a confidence and freedom that is found only through the grace of God. I am grateful to God's loving hand extending toward me during my life.

Impurity can drive us closer to God, cause us to seek out truth and clarity in life. Or it can bring about terrible confusion and devastation. When impurity touches us, we must make a quick decision to avoid spreading it. If we embrace the thoughts, even momentarily, confusion will follow. It does not take much time for a person to become defiled by impure thoughts and actions: Think, for instance, how many times in our culture entertaining a lustful thought opens a door for pornography or adultery.

Any casual statement that stretches the truth allows us to begin to embellish a story and ultimately lie. We must be very cautious, as our lives are easily influenced by the words and actions of others.

A problem occurs when we think we are right and therefore do not need to act. We might think, "Truth will eventually come out and people will see the error of their ways." Due to this mentality, we usually sit back and let the natural flow of events occur. In Germany, this is what happened. The majority of the people may not have liked what was going on, but the paralysis of impurity prevented most of them from responding. "There is nothing we can do." "If we just stay quiet, they will leave us alone." "Things will get better, eventually." I have uttered every one of those statements in my life. They are powerless, impotent thoughts that open us to mindless control by those with impurity in their spirits. It has been said, "The only thing necessary for the triumph of evil is for good men to do nothing." The violent contact of impurity confounds our thinking.

We mentioned the biblical story of David and Absalom earlier. Later events in the aftermath of that incident with another individual exemplify this chaotic mind-set.

The Impurity of Shimei

After Absalom's treason against his father, we read that David escaped from Jerusalem. He must have felt discouraged, even guilty for his son's betrayal. In his travels, King David was given the false report about Mephibosheth, Jonathan's son, which we discussed earlier. I mention it again here because it must have compounded David's sense of frustration and, perhaps, depression. It was one of those times that you might have heard King David say, "Lord, what else can go wrong today?"

What else, indeed? David rode a little farther and was confronted by Shimei, the son of Gera, from the family of the house of Saul. Imagine the number of negative comments Shimei heard about David. Having lived around Saul most of his life, Shimei must have been contaminated and polluted over and over again.

Imagine being raised in a home where negative comments are frequently made about a particular race, religion, people group or specific individuals. Do you think this would impact you? Isn't this how bias and prejudice are passed along from one generation to another? And here we have Shimei, a man from the house of Saul. Yes, King Saul, the man who attempted many times to kill David.

The following account of the meeting is a ludicrous example of a crazed man totally infected with impurity.

> [Shimei] came out, cursing continuously as he came. And he threw stones at David and at all the servants of King David. And all the people and all the mighty men were on his right hand and on his left. Also Shimei said thus when he cursed: "Come out! Come out! You bloodthirsty man, you rogue! The LORD has brought upon you all the blood of the house of Saul, in whose place you have reigned; and the LORD has delivered the kingdom into the hand of Absalom your son. So now you are caught in your own evil, because you are a bloodthirsty man!"
>
> 2 Samuel 16:5–8

Please take a minute and picture this scene. A raging man stormed toward the king, cursing him and throwing rocks at him. As if that were not enough, he challenged him and called him worthless. At the same time David was surrounded by all the people *and his mighty men*. Excuse my common language, but what kind of an idiot would do such a thing? I will tell you what kind: one who was so wrought with impurity that he was not in a rational frame of mind or thinking of consequences. Even though Shimei spoke the words, I imagine that the "spirit of Saul" was quite evident.

I love the response of Abishai, one of David's men: "Why should this dead dog curse my lord the king? Please, let me go over and take off his head!" (verse 9). David told his men to leave Shimei alone. He said that if Absalom, his own son, hated him, how much more could someone not of his flesh hate him. This response by King David was probably more a reflection of his discouragement than a desire to show mercy to an enemy. He even suggested that the Lord had ordered Shimei to curse him and added, "It may be that the LORD will look on my affliction, and that the LORD will repay me with good for his cursing this day" (verse 12). Sounds like David was having a good old-fashioned pity party.

Here we read about David, a man of God with a powerful army at his disposal, but whose own sense of confusion from Saul's and Absalom's attacks has rendered him unable to respond as a king should to such rebellion and abuse. At the same time, we see how impurity placed Shimei in a precarious position, one that led ultimately to his death. Although David spared Shimei's life at that time, one of his final instructions to Solomon, the heir to the throne, was to see that Shimei received consequences for his actions (see 1 Kings 2).

Impurity occurs when we hear evil reports with our natural ears and minds without seeking spiritual wisdom and understanding. If we accept the words of others as truth, we will become filled with a mixture of philosophies, attitudes and beliefs. "Don't be stupid and believe all you hear; be smart and know where you are headed" (Proverbs 14:15 CEV). If we listen to evil reports, we will become so filled with wrong attitudes and conclusions that we will defile everything we touch.

There are several characteristics of the track of impurity. They will help you determine whether or not impurity has gotten control of your life or someone else's life.

Characteristics of Impurity

Trusting and believing the evil report is accurate

It is crucial to protect our emotions and minds from hearing and receiving negative reports. Our tendency may be to believe the report due to past experiences or situations, but this will only open up the door to further impurity. "An evildoer gives heed to false lips" (Proverbs 17:4). Do not be one who runs *to* evil; be one who runs *from* evil.

The story of Ananias and Sapphira, found in Acts 5:1–11, gives us a clear example of how to test an evil report. Ananias stated to Peter and the apostles that he and his wife had sold a piece of land and that they were giving all of the money from the sale to the Lord. This was a lie, as they had kept back part of the proceeds. Ananias was struck dead by the Spirit of God for lying (not for withholding money). Several hours later, Sapphira came before the apostles not knowing what had happened to her husband. Peter did not assume, by the reports of Ananias, that she was guilty of deception. The Bible tells us that Peter asked her whether or not they had sold the land for the amount Ananias had indicated. She had every opportunity to be honest, explain, clarify or repent. Instead, she, too, lied and suffered the same fate as her husband. Peter, following a godly approach, did not listen to the report of Ananias, knowing he was a liar.

Peter checked it out for himself instead of passing judgment on Sapphira. As it turned out, Sapphira's words condemned her own life.

Forming negative opinions based on the report

This is a symptom of one who is infected with impurity. Our thoughts become skewed, our memories distort occurrences and we begin to think negatively about the individual. It makes no difference if we are personally involved in the situation, an observer or in a third-party discussion. We pick up the offense from another person.

While growing up, I had two very good friends named Gary and Cal. Unfortunately, they did not like one another, so the three of us seldom did anything together. Their lack of appreciation for one another stemmed from comments made by their parents. In all that Cal and Gary attempted, their fathers would compare them, boast of their exploits or encourage competition. Thus Gary and Cal formed their opinions without even getting to know one another. Sometimes I would hear one of them say something totally erroneous about the other, but not knowing how to handle it, I would laugh or ignore it. Then there were times when I found myself forming an opinion from the distorted reports shared by one friend or the other. Obviously this caused breaches in my friendships with both of them. The offense becomes ours, we personalize it and it is as if we are directly a part of the situation. "It is impossible that no offenses should come, but woe to him through whom they do come!" (Luke 17:1).

Acts 5 tells the story of Peter and the other apostles being brought before the high priest and a council of elders. Many accusations were directed toward these men of God. In the midst of the council, a man by the name of Gamaliel stood and gave guidance to the elders. He told them that if the apostles' work was simply the work of men, it would fade away. But if it was from God, the council was setting itself against an undefeatable foe. Gamaliel was saying to the people, "Don't pick up an offense. If God is a part of this and you set yourself up against Him, look out!" We must ask ourselves whether or not we are picking up an offense due to the attitudes of other people. Guard your ears and your heart from such deceptions.

Viewing an individual in a distorted perspective

Oftentimes when we believe an evil report to be true, we no longer see these people in the same way. We no longer trust them or enjoy their company. We feel they are superficial and judgmental. The areas that we once appreciated about them are no longer visible, overshadowed by our twisted thinking and contaminated spirits. Think about it—a teacher hears something negative about a student he or she will be having next year and it paints a negative impression prior to even having the child in class. Or you have new neighbors moving in next door, but a friend fills your mind with negative comments about them. Will you not be tainted? This can be deadly in a church or business setting. Where once the pastor or supervisor was seen as a trusted individual, it is now difficult to receive teaching or inspiration or counsel from him or her. I was recently talking to a member of our church who expressed just this concern about one of the elders in the church. As I explored this matter, it became clear this parishioner had an offense against the elder. The situation that had fueled the offense had been misunderstood, not interpreted correctly. (I had firsthand knowledge of the truth of the matter.) My counsel was for the person to go to the elder and ask for elucidation in the matter. I believe this will lead to clarity and a probable repentance on the part of the parishioner.

Failure to discern and question the motives of the potential false witness

This is a key test as to whether or not impurity has overtaken us: Do we interpret the reporter's words as "supporting evidence" of an infraction or do we weigh the motives? Proverbs 16:2 speaks to the core of this issue: "All the ways of a man are pure in his own eyes, but the LORD weighs the spirits [or motives]." We often naïvely assume people will be caring, honest and compassionate. Yet when people become upset or anxious about situations, a distorted view is shared with others. If I am upset with my boss, will I not share negative things? If I feel slighted by a friend, my forthcoming comments will be less than gracious.

I know of people who share their marriage difficulties with their parents or siblings. This eventually causes these in-laws to have bitter feelings toward the spouse. The results are devastating and create a barrier to reconciliation or unity within the marriage. In fact, I have seen marriages destroyed because a person has foolishly contaminated relatives this way. Think about it for a minute. If I am struggling in my marriage and tell my relatives (dad, mom, brothers, etc.) about the issues, their tendencies will be to side with me, their own flesh and blood. As this continues, their perspective will be distorted and their view of my wife will be negative. Even if things get better, it will be difficult to change the family perception of her.

If a person comes to you with a negative report, your first reaction should not be to believe it, but to look at the motivation in telling you. Why would I complain about my spouse unless I was frustrated, angry or hurt? Are people usually thinking clearly and objectively when they are in these emotional states? This leads to negative reports, distortion of facts and a sense of wanting an ally for complaints. In fact, the stronger the person speaks the false report, the more I look at his or her motives. "There is a way that seems right to a man, but its end is the way of death" (Proverbs 16:25).

Withdrawing from a person, especially in the spirit

Impurity creates a desire to distance ourselves. Whether we say that we feel uncomfortable with him or do not enjoy her company, we will limit our contact with the individual. The reality is we have become impure and taken up an offense. Again, I have noticed this within the framework of the school system, a family or a church. I have seen pastors avoid parishioners because they have held on to an evil report about them. (Embarrassingly, I admit that I have been one of those ministers.) And, likewise, I have seen people in the congregation refuse to seek prayer or spiritual support because they are angry with the pastor. People at work avoid asking for assistance from others due to an offense. And children, upset with dad or mom, no longer ask for guidance. These are clear signs of impurity.

Be sensitive to others when you see these characteristics displayed by someone. They will not be open to immediate change, and only by your careful and loving support will they come to a place of understanding. When we fall into these traps and become tainted in our perspectives, we are not bad people. It simply means we have become confused and allowed negative and critical thoughts to overcome us. There are solutions, as we have been discussing throughout this book.

In Acts 9 we read the story of Saul of Tarsus (Paul) coming to Ananias for prayer (not the same Ananias mentioned earlier about the land sale). The Lord prepared Ananias for the coming of Saul, but Ananias shared his fear of having Saul show up.

> Then Ananias answered, "Lord, I have heard from many about this man, how much harm he has done to Your saints in Jerusalem.

And here he has authority from the chief priests to bind all who call on Your name."

verses 13–14

Clearly, the reports Ananias had heard were true, but the situation had now changed. Because he held on to the information he had heard about Saul, Ananias was led to respond in impurity. Fortunately, he was able to hear the word of God and receive correction. Are you able to hear the voice of God, one that can bring clarification and truth to an impure situation?

Repeating the false report to others (being a false witness)

Naturally, if we feel justified in our emotions to withdraw, think evil of others and believe evil to be truth, it is not a large step to gossip and murmuring. Once we allow impurity to rule our lives, we become vessels for evil reports. Like magnets, we attract others, and they are drawn to us. It does not take too long before we are so confused that good looks bad and bad looks good.

We are now one step away from deception. It may seem like a long, hard journey to get there, but it happens quickly. A person who was once excited about God can become spiritually "dead" in a moment of time, if he or she allows defilement to come into his or her life. Think of it in comparison with what happens when you wash your car. You drive away from the car wash, and before you have gone a block or two, dirt settles on it. Every bird in the area recognizes the shine and glare of clean chrome as a target of defilement. Even the clouds understand that a washed car means it is time to rain. Similarly, when God washes us clean, we become greater targets for the devil. If you have allowed impurity to rule your life, get clean—that is, repent—and put on the armor of God (see Ephesians 6). Truth, righteousness, peace, faith, salvation, prayer—against these, an evil report cannot prosper or grow. Putting on the armor of God every day is essential for a strong walk in the faith.

The evil report has roared like a locomotive along six tracks. This leads us to the culmination of a defiled spirit—the place called *deception*.

EXAMINING THE HEART

1. Why do you think people hear an evil report without questioning the motives behind it?

2. Look at the characteristics of impurity again. Have you ever followed this progression in your life?

11

Walking and Speaking
in Truth

The runaway conversation has followed its destructive tracks unabated. We come now in our study to its deadly destination: deception. Once infected, an individual can no longer hold a true perspective on people and life.

The Christian community is rife with this disease, and its impact upon the Church is devastating. Until churches are willing to confront the sin of evil reporting, there will be constant divisions and factions separating people from one another and from leadership. And, of course, this problem seeps well beyond the walls of the church. Any place we repeat negative reports—the business community, schools, neighborhoods—we bring division. We open the way to dangerous terrain that may not be easily negotiated by the people involved.

Take a moment and think about your life, your sphere of influence. Where are areas of gossip most likely to be found?

Are negative comments inundating these areas of your life and impacting interactions with friends, family and colleagues? As we investigate the serious aspect of deception, evaluate your role in perpetuating critical attitudes in various arenas of your life.

Here is our working definition:

Deception: Being misled by what is false to such an extent that one does not receive or recognize guidance and truth from others.

The Bible is clear about consequences for spreading rumors. Look at these three verses from Proverbs:

- "He who repeats a matter separates friends" (17:9).
- "Whoever guards his mouth and tongue keeps his soul from troubles" (21:23).
- "A false witness will not go unpunished, and he who speaks lies shall perish" (19:9).

There is no doubt those who are pulled into deception will be manipulated; they have become pawns in the hands of the one who defiled them. We become blinded to other ideas, feedback from those around us is negated and we truly believe we have a monopoly on understanding and truth.

Many years ago, a family in the church I attended became dissatisfied with their involvement and role there. This dissatisfaction expressed itself in grumbling about the services, the music, the pastors, the youth group, etc. It was telling that when those people got upset, even minor unrelated problems became magnified. (I have seen this in marriages, in parent-child relationships and among friends.) What had been a nominal issue grew into the focal point of the situation. While the frustration of the family was real and needed to be discussed and resolved, the parents took it upon themselves to gain as many allies as possible. This took the form of phone calls, conversations with guests in their home and letters of persuasion to key individuals.

These family members used friendships and their position of influence in an attempt to alienate people from the church, from leaders and from God, as well as to justify their own beliefs and attitudes. They brought defilement upon other people and passed their disease of offense to as many as would receive it. While it was painful to see these people spread their words of poison, it was even more devastating to watch other people soak it up. Fortunately, the majority of those exposed to this tactic rejected it and confronted the people for their sin of defilement.

Unfortunately, I saw this same approach literally tear apart a school. A few of the teachers, being dissatisfied with the new principal, decided to "enlighten and educate" other teachers and parents about the problems with the administrator. It created such division in the school and community that the administrator left, many teachers transferred to other schools and even families chose to find other educational resources. I know this from a personal perspective, as I was one who transferred out of this school.

Deception can be clear and easy to spot *if* you are not the one directly involved in the deception. A little six-year-old boy once said to me, after he had been around someone rife with deception, "What's wrong with him? He seems mad at everybody." Even a child could sense and see the problems that the person would have denied vehemently.

In this chapter I will carefully explain ways to recognize deception. If, while reading, you find yourself defensive or emotionally stirred, stop and examine if there is any deception or defilement working within you. The intent of this chapter is to expose deception and help each one of us to grasp the godly principles of purity and restoration. Once again, let's look beyond pointing fingers at people and realize we have control over only one life—our own. Be responsible and evaluate your own personal life.

Signs of Deception

Sign #1: Those who are deceived point out others who are in similar deception and use them as justification for their own sins. They will use evil reports as a way to support their own deceptive patterns. This occurs frequently among groups of friends or acquaintances. An individual becomes upset with someone, targets him and shares that frustration with their social group. Then those with a tendency toward rebellion pick up on this offense as though they, too, have a grievance, and deception follows. It is not uncommon for this group to encourage or support further areas of antagonism toward the selected target. Leaders, employers, pastors, supervisors . . . beware! This behavior, when exhibited by those in authority, can do tremendous damage within businesses, homes, churches or organizations. A person who has responsibility over others also has great influence. If he or she shares a negative report with the general population, those with unguarded spirits will become contaminated.

We read about this type of defilement in the book of Esther. A man named Haman, whose position in court was above all of the princes, received a special invitation by the queen to attend a royal banquet. Unbeknownst to Haman, Esther was going to use the meal as an opportunity to expose his plan of destruction against the Jewish people. Haman, however, thought the purpose of the banquet was to honor him and to shower him with accolades.

So Haman went out that day joyful and with a glad heart; but when Haman saw Mordecai in the king's gate, and that he did not stand or tremble before him, he was filled with indignation against Mordecai.

Esther 5:9

When Haman went home, he gathered his wife and friends and told them of the honor of being asked to the banquet. He also shared his anger and frustration with Mordecai, who was a Jew. In fact, he stated emphatically that even though a great honor was being given to him, it was of no significance because of the disdain and dishonor he believed was shown him by Mordecai.

Haman's wife and friends wanted to please him, to revel in his glory, perhaps even to receive some of his upcoming riches. Joining Haman's complaint willingly, their own rebellious, dishonest hearts became exposed.

> Then his wife Zeresh and all his friends said to him, "Let a gallows be made, fifty cubits high, and in the morning suggest to the king that Mordecai be hanged on it; then go merrily with the king to the banquet." And the thing pleased Haman; so he had the gallows made.

Esther 5:14

The pattern is clear: An evil report is given, and people align themselves with the "offended" individual and become defiled. In turn, in their own deception, they become a part of the murmuring and gossip. Haman's "friends" added fuel to the fire of defilement.

When the time of the banquet arrived, Queen Esther told the king of Haman's plan. The king was furious. Though Haman begged for his life, he was hanged on the very gallows he had built for Mordecai. The estate of Haman was then given over to Queen Esther. What Satan so often intends as evil, God turns toward the good of His people.

167

There are consequences and repercussions for impurity, defilement, lies and deception. These occur in both the natural and spiritual realms. In the natural life, for instance, there may be a lack of trust. Is there anyone who enjoys being lied to? A false story will create a barrier between people very quickly. And as in the natural realm, deception creates spiritual barriers. Only this time it separates us from God and the ability to be guided by the Holy Spirit. Do not allow yourself to become deceived by taking on another person's offense or complaint.

I speak a strong word of caution to husbands and wives, significant others and close family members. We often take on the offense when a loved one is wronged or slighted. And though they may work through the issue, we still hold on to the anger and bitterness.

Sign #2: Those who are deceived actively seek out false or evil reports about others. This person might resemble a news reporter when interviewing and questioning others in an effort to garner negative information about a person or situation. Or perhaps a better illustration is that of an archaeologist digging up old artifacts and bones, trying to piece together occurrences from the past. "An ungodly man digs up evil, and it is on his lips like a burning fire" (Proverbs 16:27). Beware of this type of person, as he will surely influence you and create confusion in your life. The picture he paints seems real and accurate, yet underneath, the canvas is one of deception and dishonesty.

The Pharisees and the religious people were chronically attempting to "dig up" information to be used against Jesus.

> Now it happened, as Jesus sat at the table in the house, that behold, many tax collectors and sinners came and sat down with Him and His disciples. And when the Pharisees saw it, they said to His disciples, "Why does your Teacher eat with tax collectors and sinners?"
>
> Matthew 9:10–11

And when the Pharisees saw it [the disciples eating in the grainfield on the Sabbath], they said to Him, "Look, Your disciples are doing what is not lawful to do on the Sabbath!"

Matthew 12:2

And behold, there was a man who had a withered hand. And they asked Him, saying, "Is it lawful to heal on the Sabbath?"—that they might accuse Him. . . . Then the Pharisees went out and plotted against Him, how they might destroy Him.

Matthew 12:10, 14

A person in deception must justify his stance and beliefs continually. If he should stop and truly examine what is occurring, he would have to admit his faults and wrong perspective. Perhaps incapable because of an unrepentant heart, the individual continues a life of deception and defilement.

I have a friend who was deeply wounded at work by her supervisor, and though the incident occurred close to ten years ago, she occasionally ruminates on the hurt and frustration of this event. She periodically connects with former colleagues and will ask questions about her former supervisor and look for areas of problems at the workplace. With her emotions beginning to bubble up, she appears to conjure up past anger and bitterness toward this employer. She uses current issues, problems and frustrations that others experience to validate her own previous incidents at work. She does not see any harm in this, though it creates ongoing emotional struggles in her life and influences her current attitude at her new workplace.

Sign #3: Those who are deceived seek out others to agree with them. This was discussed earlier as we studied the life of Absalom. Through rationalization and manipulation Absalom was able to justify his own position of usurping the authority from King David. There is tremendous strength and power when we join forces with others. This is what Korah did to Moses, what Absalom did to David and what the religious people did to Jesus. Another powerful example is seen in Acts 23, where we read about a group of Jewish people who joined forces to kill the apostle Paul.

> And when it was day, some of the Jews banded together and bound themselves under an oath, saying that they would neither eat nor drink till they had killed Paul. Now there were more than forty who had formed this conspiracy.
>
> Acts 23;12–13

We have heard it said, "There is safety in numbers." This is the essence of those in deception. The more people they can rally to their sides, the more confident they become. An interesting side note: Either these people in Acts 23 all died of starvation or they broke their vow, as they did not kill Paul. In this area of deception, we often make foolish comments and commitments that we later wish to reconsider.

Sign #4: Those who are deceived believe they are doing the will of God by coming against others. A posture of self-righteousness, of arrogance clouds the mind of the deceived and justifies attacks on others because of their faults and sins. A person may feel that he is God's instrument of judgment or vengeance. This is very dangerous, as the individual may consider himself above the law—morally, ethically or otherwise. Remember how King Saul justified his own agenda by modifying the directions of God (see 1 Samuel 13, 15). Saul's life was full of contradictions and deceptions. He spent many years trying to kill David, the one who had been anointed by God to succeed him to the throne. While this sign of deception is often blatant, it does not have to be. Subtle behaviors—a negative word about a co-worker, a false story about a peer or "friend," the evil report about leadership—these are the ways of potential deception.

I believe we have all had the experience of being verbally attacked and assaulted by another individual. This is especially difficult when the attack comes from a family member or friend. Psalm 55 speaks of the hurt caused by friends who turn against us.

> For it is not an enemy who reproaches me; then I could bear it. Nor is it one who hates me who has exalted himself against me; then I could hide from him. But it was you, a man my equal, my companion and my acquaintance. We took sweet counsel together, and walked to the house of God in the throng.
>
> verses 12–14

The subject of God's people coming against one another is of grave concern to many in the church community. Entire church denominations refuse to fellowship with one another because of differences in doctrine or practice. One church promotes contemporary music while another uses hymns. One congregation may dance in praise and worship of God with lifted hands. Another congregation may sit quietly and reverently during worship and during the sermons, without an amen or hallelujah being uttered. When we let these differences separate us from one another, we are standing in judgment and moving toward deception. The poor testimony and witness of Christians against Christians has occurred in such epic proportions that many unbelievers use the word *hypocritical* to describe the church world. Each judgmental group feels that it has heard from God and is, therefore, justified to promote an evil report.

And this naturally extends beyond the walls of a church. I see strong political comments from those with contrary beliefs as if the opposing sides were locked in a literal fight to the death. And, comically, there are many whose views change every few years, depending on funding and the political rhetoric of their party affiliation. We believe we are so right that no other view can be evaluated objectively. Be careful how strongly you "dig in" on a perspective. You may change your mind in the coming days, weeks or years. Going back and admitting your change in attitude may be somewhat difficult or embarrassing.

Naturally, there are perspectives and beliefs that we all feel very strongly about in our lives. One may present an alternative or contrary approach and it may not take much time for the person to evaluate. Some personal convictions have been established after much soul-searching, studying and experiences that have led one to conclude that this "truth" is right. Be sensitive to people in this area, as attempts to change their minds or push them other directions may be met with resistance. This does not mean they are in deception as much as it means they have strong convictions.

Sign #5: Those who are deceived refuse to receive counsel because "everyone else is wrong." If an individual becomes so confident in "self" that she refuses to listen to others, deception may be upon her. "Where there is no counsel, the people fall; but in the multitude of counselors there is safety" (Proverbs 11:14).

One year ago a woman we know was planning to get married and contacted me. Jenny had been married several times before; each time the relationship had ended in divorce, multiplying her emotional scars. She had several children from these marriages. Jenny was now planning on getting married again. My wife and I had met with her for counseling many times over the years. As I met with her this time, it was evident that she did not want my counsel or guidance, but she did want my blessing and excitement on her upcoming marriage. She admitted that a number of other people had discouraged her from going forth with this endeavor. I told Jenny that I agreed with the others' discernment and encouraged her to have premarital counseling. She got upset and told me that I did not understand. She had "heard from God" and was to get married.

Jenny got married the next week. Within a month, I received a call from Jenny and her new husband for marriage counseling. The next few months were filled with phone calls and counseling appointments. Despite numerous interventions, the marriage failed.

Jenny is not a bad person for choosing the directions she has in life. She desired something good (marriage), but was unwilling to prepare appropriately. Her selfish desires were placed above the counsel of her friends and family. People in deception will often say they have heard from God but cannot explain why others have heard something different. Those giving counsel are usually friends, family, spiritual leaders or accountability partners. Suddenly all these people "do not understand the situation." It is frightening when an individual thinks she is the only one who can hear from God. This isolationist mentality leads to withdrawal, as we will see in our next sign of deception. Decisions are then based on emotions rather than on the Spirit of God. "The way of a fool is right in his own eyes, but he who heeds counsel is wise" (Proverbs 12:15).

This "I am right and everyone else is wrong" attitude permeates the world. We see people in sports, music, the arts and theater, the political arena, our own workplace, family or neighborhood that have this same approach to life. On a recent birthday, I gave my wife a card that stated on the outside, "You are a success because you live by one golden rule," and then inside it said, "It's my way or the highway." While this was just a joke with my wife (really, honey, just a joke!), it is unfortunately a truth in many lives.

Sign #6: Those who are deceived isolate themselves from godly contacts with friends, family and leadership. Think about it. Why would a person who is self-focused, self-centered or in rebellion want to be around people who are challenging him to seek God for guidance? When you see a person pulling back, refusing fellowship with friends and family, isolating himself from the Word of God, watch out! This is a person who may be walking on the road of deception.

Stephen is a young man I know who, at one time, had felt a deep love for God and the family of God. In recent years, however, his focus began to shift toward his career. Understandably, to be effective at his job and receive promotions, he needed to give it his attention and energy, but as time went on work began to conflict more and more with his commitment to his faith. Stephen is no longer connected with his Christian friends because he gives his time almost exclusively to his work. His family, of course, has been affected by this, as well. A decision to remove oneself from God's life-giving presence cannot help but affect others.

Some of his friends tried to approach him and explain what they saw as the beginning of imbalance in his life. This concern was not well received. He poured more and more time into his career. Stephen used to read the Bible, pray and seek Christian relationships. He now finds other sources of connection. In his words, "I just don't have anything in common with the people in church."

I still have hope and faith that Stephen will see what has become of his life—his isolation and his refusal to interact with God's people, the very ones who could speak life to him. "A man who isolates himself seeks his own desire; he rages against all wise judgment" (Proverbs 18:1).

Unfortunately, we see this same pattern develop for those who have addictive personalities. They begin to be drawn back into the darkness of their addiction (drugs, gambling, pornography, etc.), and they isolate themselves from others in life. Soon they have insulated their lives, like a cocoon, and are not able to be touched by the love and compassion of friends and family.

Deception in Action

A person may exhibit any number of these signs of deception—rebellion, isolation, defiance, etc. I want to conclude this chapter with an example of a person who (I can see with hindsight) was strongly deceived and drawn into many of these behaviors. See if you recognize any of them.

After I graduated from college, I worked as a counselor at a state correctional facility for juveniles. The children in the facility ranged from ages ten to eighteen and were incarcerated for sentences of up to two and a half years. This was a secure, locked facility with a constant security patrol. It was not unheard of for a resident to try to escape.

The senior counselor, Joan, had been there for many years. She was a seasoned veteran whom the residents did not tangle with. She had applied for numerous supervisory positions but had not been promoted. This had caused bitterness to build up within her, which manifested itself through derogatory remarks about the supervisors, comments of "better" ways to do things. Gradually, Joan began a covert stirring of insurrection among the residents. Joan would tell a resident that he was being treated too harshly and that she would talk to the supervisor about it. She would then approach various employees with suggestions for changes and ask for their support in upcoming staff meetings. Joan soon became the champion of the residents and the mouthpiece for the staff. In a prison-type setting, this is not good—as one can imagine.

Because Joan and I were assigned to the same cottage, we worked together frequently. She was friendly toward me. She helped me through orientation and would "guide" me in my daily activities. Personally, as a 23-year-old young adult, I appreciated her concern and input as my experiences were limited. This is a nice way of saying I was naïve and immature.

As the months passed, I also became friends with one of the other counselors, Martin, and with our supervisor, Pat. We played basketball and worked out together. Unfortunately, Joan was upset with both Martin and Pat. She was jealous of Pat's supervisory status and of Martin's close relationship with him. As time went on, Joan began to make negative comments to me about Pat. She questioned decisions he made and suggested alternative solutions. "If only I were the supervisor!" echoed faintly through her comments. Then she began to warn me about Martin. When I was paired with him on a day shift, she pointed out possible problems that might develop. In time, I began to eye my friends with wariness and hesitancy.

One day Pat and I were playing football with the residents on the courtyard beside the cottage. While it was required that a staff person always be in the cottage, the day was beautiful and all the residents were with us. Because I was with my supervisor, I did not give it much more thought. We enjoyed a game of football for about 45 minutes and then returned to the cottage for our daily chores.

When I arrived at work the next day, I was summoned to the office of the superintendent of the facility. I had never been in Dr. Ransly's office and was quite nervous about being called to meet with him. When I arrived my heart sank. There, along with the superintendent, were the case manager of the facility and a sheepish-looking Pat.

Dr. Ransly began to speak, a stern look on his face. "Mike, with more than two hundred adolescents in this facility, it is important for all of us to follow the same rules. Would you agree?" I responded in the affirmative, trying to piece things together. Questions raced through my mind, but I said nothing.

Gradually I began to understand; the proverbial light bulb went on. Joan had tried to call the cottage the day before when we were outside playing football and had received no response. We learned later that she had then contacted security and had been informed that Pat and I were with the residents playing football outside. She had chosen at that point to call the superintendent's office and express alarm that there was no answer at the cottage. She had said she was concerned because the rules were clear that a supervisor was supposed to be there all day.

My discipline was a written reprimand and a feeling of embarrassment. Joan feigned ignorance as to her motivation, simply saying she called because she was worried something had happened in the cottage. The spider had woven the web and the flies had been caught.

As I recall this incident, Joan's motivation and intentions are easy to see. Joan had been injured by rejection in her personal and professional life. Though she had a place of responsibility and recognition, she wanted more. I was caught in the middle between her and Pat, the one she had targeted. Her willingness to help me and give me guidance appeared genuine yet was actually a part of her need to control and groom me for her own support and advancement. She wanted people to agree with her, not grow.

Over the next months Joan's depth of impurity and deception became evident. She withdrew from people and openly stirred up strife among the residents and counselors. Her refusal to look at her own life and to actively pursue truth created a barrier in all her relationships. Eventually, she was transferred to another cottage, but she soon left.

People who operate in deception may be helpful, caring and pleasant to be around when everything is going their way. But if someone or something takes a turn contrary to their desires, the sheep turns into a wolf quickly.

Our Hope?

Deception is a one-way ticket to spiritual death. Deception, like a giant boa constrictor, will suffocate and squeeze the very life out of a person. He will feel the pressure, the spiritual life flowing out, but he will be so bound by the coils of deception it will seem easier to give up than to fight. People in deception argue, attack, become embittered and eventually grow weary and fall into a lifeless routine without any hope of change.

A bleak and depressing picture? Yes, it is. Fortunately, it is not a pre-determined fate. We have all fallen prey to impurity and deception. It is not a life sentence if we remain open to hearing from others around us. Seek God's wisdom and understanding above your own.

For others—be kind and sensitive, and have empathy. Be willing to walk with them (for a time) through their impurity and deception, but place clear and firm boundaries on the conversations. In time, it may be necessary to minimize contact or communication with the person. That is naturally a personal decision, but one that may be important for your own emotional and spiritual health.

For ourselves—be willing to receive counsel. Ask those whom you trust for feedback and perspective. Seek counsel from more experienced people. Watch your words and attitude as you express your feelings and thoughts. And remember, if you want to always be right, only listen to yourself. That is, you can fool yourself into thinking you are always right. Remember Proverbs 18:1: "It's selfish and stupid to think only of yourself and to sneer at people who have sense. Fools have no desire to learn; they would much rather give their own opinion" (CEV).

Fortunately, we serve a God of second chances. Even though we may have journeyed into areas of confusion or impurity or even deception, the cleansing process of the Holy Spirit can reach each part of our lives. What an awesome and powerful God! He cares deeply for His people.

===== EXAMINING THE HEART =====

1. Do any of the signs of deception show up in your life? If so, which ones?

2. If you have recognized any symptoms of deception creeping into the life of a friend or family member, how might you address the situation?

3. Are you keeping company with people who are in deception? Are there "companions" in your life that interfere with accomplishing all of God's plan for you?

12

The Cleansing Process

Dear Lord, so far today, I've done all right. I haven't gossiped, haven't lost my temper, haven't been greedy, grumpy, nasty, selfish or overindulgent. I'm really glad about that. But in a few minutes, God, I'm going to get out of bed, and from then on, I'm probably going to need a lot more help. Thank You. In Jesus' name, Amen.

Do you feel this way some days? This prayer might seem particularly relevant when we consider how easy it is to walk headlong into an evil report. Nevertheless, if you have been sucked into runaway conversations, there are two options. You can stay in bed and pull the covers over your head, or you can read on and learn about the cleansing process God has for us when we have been defiled. Let's "get out of bed" and face squarely whatever God has for us today.

"I don't wanna get washed up. I'm not dirty. I didn't play with any germs." How many of us said this when we were younger and now hear it from our children? It is indeed amazing how my son can play basketball for so many hours yet never get dirty. His insistence that "I didn't sweat" or that "I only touched the ball with my hands" is comical. Recently I was in a store and the person next to me in line had a very pungent odor. As I watched others react with wrinkled-up noses, looks of disgust or even disbelief, I felt sure the shopper was not aware of giving off an offensive smell. This is how deception affects us in life. We do not recognize the filth on our bodies or the foul odor we are giving off.

This recognition or perception is affected by other factors. For example, if I have finished mowing the lawn but plan to continue working outside, I will not feel the need to shower and change. If I am going to meet some friends at a movie, however, I will get cleaned up (much to the relief of my friends). As long as I am going to be around "dirt," why clean up? In fact, when I am in the midst of dirt and grime, I may not even recognize how dirty I am. A group of skunks may be quite comfortable with the smell of one another, but include a cat in the group and at least one animal will be unhappy.

How does this relate to the area of defilement?

Marvin had a circle of co-workers who spoke negatively about their supervisor. At first it did not seem like a big deal. He enjoyed work and liked his employer. But in time, Marvin found that he, too, was frustrated with the supervisor's attitude and lack of compassion. He began to comment about how she only came out of her office to complain and yell. Marvin's wife pointed out his change in attitude, but he minimized the problem. There are usually people attempting to warn us about becoming polluted, but our self-centered nature keeps us from hearing them. "Whoever loves instruction loves knowledge, but he who hates correction is stupid" (Proverbs 12:1).

Marvin needed to get "cleaned up" from the defiling conversation poured out by his fellow employees. What prevented

Marvin, and others like him, from becoming cleansed from the pollution? It was his decision to continue to engage in negative conversation with his colleagues. If our perception is that we are only going to get dirty again or that we do not need to be clean for the next job we do, there is no motivation for purification. Unless Marvin saw that his conversations with his co-workers kept him defiled, he would not desire a change. As long as the group was homogenous, the "smell" would never be identified. They needed someone to stand up and proclaim the conversation foul. They needed someone like you, an individual who understands the implications of listening to negative conversations. If even one person stands up and makes a plea for cleanliness in a conversation, it can drastically change the course of future discussions.

Is becoming cleansed as easy as saying, "I'm dirty and want to be cleansed"? Let me give a definitive answer: yes and no. We can answer yes in that God is able to come and purify us with a fresh breath from the Holy Spirit. We can also say no, however, because any cleansing or healing received must be walked out. Does an alcoholic person become clean by admitting she is an alcoholic or by staying sober? Does an adulterer become purified by confessing the sinful action or by true repentance, turning from the behavior 180 degrees? It is important to recognize our condition, our sin. Yet this recognition must be coupled with prayer, guidance, action, faith, direction.

Am I Leprous?

There was a man in the Old Testament who was defiled. He was dirty, smelly and impure. He could not run away from it, nor could he become clean on his own. He admitted his impurity, yet each day it remained with him. No amount of hiding it, telling people about it or denying it changed the fact that this man was defiled and soon to become an outcast. However, a young stranger spoke a word of truth to this man. She told of a way to become cleansed, a way that would take him down a path contrary to any he had been down before. He had a choice to make—whether to become bitter and offended at his lot in life or to pursue a cleansing process. Which path did he follow? Let's read the story of Naaman, the leper.

Now Naaman, commander of the army of the king of Syria, was a great and honorable man in the eyes of his master, because by him the LORD had given victory to Syria. He was also a mighty man of valor, but a leper. And the Syrians had gone out on raids, and had brought back captive a young girl from the land of Israel. She waited on Naaman's wife. Then she said to her mistress, "If only my master were with the prophet who is in Samaria! For he would heal him of his leprosy." And Naaman went in and told his master, saying, "Thus and thus said the girl who is from the land of Israel." Then the king of Syria said, "Go now, and I will send a letter to the king of Israel." So he departed and took with him ten talents of silver, six thousand shekels of gold, and ten changes of clothing. Then he brought the letter to the king of Israel, which said, "Now be advised, when this letter comes to you, that I have sent Naaman my servant to you, that you may heal him of his leprosy."

And it happened, when the king of Israel read the letter, that he tore his clothes and said, "Am I God, to kill and make alive, that this man sends a man to me to heal him of his leprosy? Therefore please consider, and see how he seeks a quarrel with me." So it was, when Elisha the man of God heard that the king of Israel had torn his clothes, that he sent to the king, saying, "Why have you torn your clothes? Please let him come to me, and he shall know that there is a prophet in Israel." Then Naaman went with his horses and chariot, and he stood at the door of Elisha's house. And Elisha sent a messenger to him, saying, "Go and wash in the Jordan seven times, and your flesh shall be restored to you, and you shall be clean."

But Naaman became furious, and went away and said, "Indeed, I said to myself, 'He will surely come out to me, and stand and call on the name of the LORD his God, and wave his hand over the place, and heal the leprosy.' Are not the Abanah and the Pharpar, the rivers of Damascus, better than all the waters of Israel? Could I not wash in them and be clean?" So he turned and went away in a rage. And his servants came near and spoke to him, and said, "My father, if the prophet had told you to do something great, would you not have done it? How much more then, when he says to you, 'Wash, and be clean'?" So he went down and dipped seven times in the Jordan, according to the saying of the man of God; and his flesh was restored like the flesh of a little child, and he was clean.

And he returned to the man of God, he and all his aides, and came and stood before him; and he said, "Indeed, now I know that there is no God in all the earth, except in Israel; now therefore, please take a gift from your servant." But he said, "As the LORD lives, before whom I stand, I will receive nothing." And he urged him to take, but he refused. So Naaman said, "Then, if not, please let your servant be given two mule-loads of earth; for your servant will no longer offer either burnt offering or sacrifice to other gods, but to the LORD. Yet in this thing may the LORD pardon your servant: when my master goes into the temple of Rimmon to worship there, and he leans on my hand, and I bow down in the temple of Rimmon—when I bow down in the temple of Rimmon, may the LORD please pardon your servant in this thing." Then he said to him, "Go in peace."

2 Kings 5:1–18

I believe that Naaman exhibits the way that cleansing from defilement in the natural (or physical) parallels cleansing from defilement in the spiritual. He had many obstacles to overcome—distance, finances, communication, anger, pride and disillusionment to name a few. Does this list look familiar? These are the very things that prevented others (Judas, Absalom, King Saul . . .) from achieving freedom from deception.

Attempts to bring restoration to an individual who has fallen into deception will usually be unsuccessful unless he or she addresses the area of being polluted by an evil report. Once this is acknowledged, repented of and prayed for, the Holy Spirit can bring forgiveness, love, humility, understanding and guidance to the person. I know this seems like a strong statement, but Scripture bears this out:

> To the pure all things are pure, but to those who are defiled and unbelieving nothing is pure; but even their mind and conscience are defiled. They profess to know God, but in works they deny Him, being abominable, disobedient, and disqualified for every good work.
>
> Titus 1:15–16

Now *that* is a strong statement! Let's examine, step-by-step, what Naaman did to obtain his healing and cleansing in life.

Apprehending Cleansing in Your Life

1. Naaman recognized his condition. Now, you might say, "Of course, Naaman recognized his condition! It was obvious: There is no denying the flaky skin, swelling and sores of leprosy. My 'condition,' my sin, however, is minor. No one notices it. It is easy to hide."

Is it? Does sin go unnoticed? The reality is that people can see our defilement: They can smell it; they hear it; they touch and taste it. The real question is not "Do other people see my defilement?" but "Do I see my own defilement?" How long had Naaman been leprous? How long had he been hiding the sores under his clothing, his armor? Was he so defiled that he was unable to be intimate with his wife and family? Did his peers and his servants whisper, "Unclean, unclean," when he walked among them? How much longer would it have been before Naaman's skin had rotted away completely, before his nose or his ear had fallen off?

A servant girl spoke a word to Naaman's wife, who shared it with Naaman. Together, in unity, they took hold of the word and confronted his leprosy. What other choice did he have? You see, the "living dead" have no future. If you are leprous from gossiping and murmuring, you are rotting away spiritually. As Naaman did, admit your condition of defilement. Confront your sin. This is the first step toward cleansing.

2. Naaman had a desire to be cleansed. In verse 4 we read how Naaman approached his master regarding his situation. Naaman, being a man under authority, understood the importance of approaching higher power. When we are feeling overwhelmed, confronted by a problem beyond our comprehension, do we approach others for guidance, support and direction?

Simply having a desire for something is not enough. If Naaman had only had a desire, but no understanding of authority, he might have left on his own, no kingly letter in his hand, and walked boldly, even brazenly, into the court of the king of Israel. Minimally, Naaman would have been laughed out of Israel for such presumption, but most likely he would have been killed for dishonoring and insulting the king. There are usually many obstacles to achieving cleansing in a life. Desire alone is not enough. What else is needed to receive a total cleansing from God?

3. Naaman would not be distracted from receiving his cleansing. Have you ever mapped out a plan in your mind, known exactly how it should occur, what was to be said and how you would respond? Yes, it was a great plan, but there was one small problem: It did not happen the way you thought it should. Unfulfilled expectation can create disappointment and hurt feelings.

Recently Joyce and I planned to go out for the evening. All day we talked about how nice the dinner was going to be and how we were looking forward to just relaxing and talking with one another. As we were almost ready to walk out the door, we got a phone call from a couple in our church. Their son had been in an accident and was at the hospital. The doctors were considering emergency surgery. For the next hour or two I encouraged and prayed with this couple at the hospital. When I returned home it was too late to go out. Our "beautiful dream" evening was over. The next couple of hours were not very pleasant in our home. Both of us were grumpy and impatient. As the evening neared an end, however, we began talking and realized that our frustration was neither at each other nor at the couple who had called. It was the disappointment of not having our plans for the evening fulfilled. We were frustrated over our unfulfilled dreams.

Naaman faced great disappointment. He assumed that all he had to do was take a letter to the king and he would receive a healing. But the king was far from excited to see Naaman. In fact he was angry, believing Naaman was trying to provoke a war by embarrassing him. The king tore his clothes, as a sign of mourning, and accused Naaman of an ulterior military motive. The king rejected Naaman's plea for help and probably had him removed from his presence.

This was the critical time for Naaman. Would he return home, defeated and downcast? Would he leave Israel speaking evil of the king for refusing to help a commander from a neighboring land? Naaman stood at a crossroads in his life.

What would you have done? How do you respond when you do not get your way? Do you become disillusioned or discouraged? Do you allow God to direct your words and your course of action? We often fall into traps (or patterns) that prevent us from hearing God's voice. Until we break these patterns, our cleansing will be delayed or will be only temporary.

Elisha heard about the matter and chose to intercede. Elisha told the king that Naaman should come see him so that "he shall know that there is a prophet in Israel" (2 Kings 5:8). What boldness and confidence Elisha had in God! This was not the voice of arrogance declaring, "I can do it!" This was a humble servant who knew what his God could do in the life of a submitted man. So the message went forth for Naaman.

I have often wondered how long it took for these messages to travel. Think about it. How long after the king tore his clothes did Elisha find out about it? An hour? A day? A week? Then how long before Elisha responded to the situation with a message to the king? Another day? Two days? Or more? Remember, there were no quick phone calls. Elisha could not be contacted via a website such as www.prophet.com.

This information transaction could have taken days or even weeks. The Bible does not tell us the time frame, but I believe it is a significant point to ponder. Naaman, hurt, wounded, rejected, disappointed, was still in the area. He had not left to go home and wallow in self-pity. No, Naaman wanted a miracle and was bound and determined to apprehend his cleansing. He must have been waiting—waiting for the right direction, guidance and purpose. He knew what he wanted and would *not* be distracted.

4. Naaman overcame his pride and his fears. This next section of Naaman's story reminds me of the sign that says, "What part of the word *no* don't you understand?" The instructions were plain and clear: "Go wash in the Jordan seven times and you will be cleansed." After all those years of being leprous, of being embarrassed and afraid to have people touch him, Naaman was "seven dips" away from being restored to purity.

The Hebrew word for *clean* in this passage is *taher*. *Strong's Concordance* (#2891) shows this word to mean "sound, clear, unadulterated, uncontaminated, innocent and pure, self-cleansing and purging." Elisha was offering Naaman a new start. We are not talking here about a "quick rinse at the car wash" cleansing, but a "stripped, repainted, super buff shine" cleansing. And all he had to do was follow the instructions of the prophet of God.

And yet this great, honorable man who was commander of the king of Syria's army responded with fury (see verse 11). The word used for his anger means to "burst out in rage." Why was Naaman so angry? Was he upset that he was asked to bathe in the dirty waters of the Jordan River—waters that could not compare to the clear rivers of his homeland?

Did he expect more than he got from Elisha? Elisha did not meet with Naaman personally; he sent his messenger. Was Naaman offended by this? Perhaps he had heard about the scene on Mount Carmel between Elisha's predecessor and teacher, Elijah, and the prophets of Baal. Did Naaman expect lightning, trumpets and a heavenly pronouncement of his healing? Had he built his case as one of great importance?

Or was Naaman perhaps starting to have doubts and fears about whether or not it could really happen to him? Many times I find that people who have tremendous faith for others find it difficult to have faith for their own miracles. "I know God can heal my friend's marriage, but I don't know about mine." "Yes, I believe God has financial provision for people, but as for me . . ." Could Naaman have begun to doubt God's intervention in his life? Regardless of his inner struggles, Naaman still desired cleansing, so he let his pride—and his fears—be brought into the light.

5. Naaman was willing to receive counsel, correction and direction from others. In the midst of his frustration and anger, Naaman was willing to hear the voice of others. This is a key point. Most likely, there will be multiple obstacles and barriers to the cleansing process. Why? If we are defiled and dirty we can offer little testimony to the world. Once cleansed, however, we exhibit a great deal about the power of God and thus become targets for every demonic force of Satan: "Your enemy, the devil, is like a roaring lion, sneaking around to find someone to attack" (1 Peter 5:8 CEV).

It is very difficult to "have ears that hear" at this point in the process. First of all, we do not see ourselves as defiled or polluted. We think we are right and can handle everything ourselves. We are suspicious about counsel. We question the motives of those giving it. We actually fight the process of cleansing using words such as *manipulating, self-centered* and *controlling* to describe the interventions of others. We accuse even our closest friends and supporters of being insensitive and uncaring. Whereas once we received challenges and guidance from others, now we meet each comment or suggestion with disdain and animosity. It is during this phase that people have a tendency to reject the process of cleansing, choosing instead to walk away from purity and to blame and curse others for their lack of support and love.

It can be difficult to respond to direction when we have a different perspective on the problem. Some years ago, I was in a staff meeting and expressed a viewpoint that was in the minority. In fact it was such a minority viewpoint that I was the only one who agreed with it. This should have been my first clue that, perhaps, I needed to pray and rethink my view. Instead, I decided that everyone else needed enlightenment. I had acted on impulse in a situation, without getting counsel, and my colleagues were asking me to explain the motivation behind my actions. The more I talked, however, the more confusing the situation became. I found myself feeling isolated, defensive and somewhat frustrated that my fellow ministers did not "get it."

As the conversation continued, the Lord began to speak to me regarding my pride and my refusal to receive correction. At that point I repented and asked forgiveness from the staff for my independent attitudes. I saw that the problem was not in my differing opinion but in the way I expressed that opinion and did not give credence to other ideas. Admittedly, this was difficult for my pride and ego. I do not like to make mistakes (who does?), and I especially do not like seeing the fleshly spirit of independence in my life.

In the days to come, through a running dialogue with my wife and a close friend, I saw the tendency I have to react to situations. When I think I have an answer or direction, I will move toward a resolution. This can create an independent, isolating spirit that gives the impression that I do not need people, that "my own competence" is sufficient to go it alone. In this regard Joyce needs to remind me of communicating and being a "team player" in our marriage.

I am thankful that I have accountability to other people who are faithful to help me break these holds on my life. How about you? Are there others on whom you can rely to speak honestly to you? Do you *allow* them to speak to you?

Naaman, the commander of an army, was used to making independent decisions quickly, with little input. Yet he was open to counsel and guidance. His independent nature was suppressed, and he listened to those who surrounded him. It saved his life and opened up a new destiny for him and his family. If you find yourself identifying with the tendency to isolate and refuse the counsel of others, make the decision to open yourself to other people. Contact several friends and verbally commit to accountability with them. Do not wait; do it now!

When Naaman began to walk the path toward cleansing, he was confronted by a king who tried to pick a fight. While struggling with rejection and discouragement, Naaman's spirit was lifted by a message from Elisha. Soon his soaring spirit was dashed by the prospect that Elisha would not meet with him.

With this offense brewing in his soul, the request made of him felt like a final crushing blow. Surely he could wash in the rivers of his hometown under much "cleaner" circumstances. In his own mind, Naaman must have had many "better ideas" than washing in the river. There will be no end of influences to help close our ears to the process of cleansing. Satan does not want us to be clean, but *God does*: "In the world you will have tribulation; but be of good cheer, I have overcome the world" (John 16:33). Naaman listened to good counsel and was able to confront his flesh, his doubts and his anger and pursue cleansing. What a tremendous model of perseverance and determination he is to all of us! Naaman passed the test. He overcame the obstacles. He was now ready to take a step of faith, one that would lead him to a brand-new life.

6. **Naaman was obedient and submitted to a higher authority.** The direction or counsel to wash in the Jordan did not come from his colleagues and servants. No, their counsel was to listen to the higher authority, Elisha the prophet. If Elisha had said, "Jump three times and then stand on one leg," their counsel would have been the same. Naaman chose to come under and respond to the authority that was before him. He asked for input and now needed to receive the instruction.

Naaman went and dipped himself in the Jordan River. The Bible says that "his flesh was restored like the flesh of a little child, and he was clean" (2 Kings 5:14). What an incredible sight that must have been! Yet the people carried away with them something more impressive still: the life lesson that Naaman modeled in seeking cleansing, fighting off resistance, receiving counsel and submitting to authority.

Is that the end of the story? For a momentary cleansing, yes, that is the end of the road. However, if we desire to walk in a permanent victory and not fall back into a "leprous" situation, there is one final step.

7. Naaman repented and took a stand toward righteousness.
He left no doors open. He was cleansed but did not want to lose
his healing. How many times have you had a breakthrough in
a spiritual area only to lose it in the coming days due to anger,
jealousy, arrogance, pride or any other number of sinful traps?
This is not only frustrating, but often becomes discouraging.
By taking the next step, Naaman was able to break this fleshly
pattern and make a statement of permanence.

So what did Naaman do to prevent his seeds of cleansing
from being washed away? He repented and then took a stand
for righteousness by making godly declarations over his life.

We have to keep a vigilant eye on our progress. Think of it
this way. Each year my family plants a garden in our backyard.
We plant tomatoes, squash, zucchini, spinach, raspberries, pep-
pers, pumpkins and anything else we may get excited about that
particular year. One year we planted the garden and began the
wait in anticipation of a beautiful harvest. Several days after
planting, however, it began to rain. For the next week or so, the
sun was nowhere to be found as the skies poured down water.
When the deluge finally relented, our beautifully planted garden
was a swampland. Many seeds had washed away, and those that
remained rotted out in a few weeks. The only answer was to
replant the garden.

What are we doing to prevent the seed of purification from
being deadened by the downpour of discouragement? Are we
taking steps to ensure that our cleansing will take root in our
spirits? If you have lost your healing, your cleansing, because
of the downpour from the clouds of life, the answer may be
to replant your seeds. It does take extra time and energy, but it
is the only way to yield a harvest if your first planting is lost.

The next several verses record Naaman's declaration that he
would serve only God. He would no longer sacrifice to idols. He
explained that by virtue of his job (the king used Naaman as a

physical support to lean on), he would have to enter the pagan temples and kneel. But he asked the Lord's forgiveness in advance for any improprieties in this area. While the Bible does not tell us what took place when Naaman returned, I believe that God provided a way to spare him the indignities of bowing down before those idols. Who knows? As a new believer, Naaman may have brought salvation to his entire family. Regardless, Naaman chose to exalt God for the healing and verbally declared the greatness of the Lord. He chose humility and faithfulness for his life and proclaimed a pathway to righteousness. Naaman would no longer be known as a leper; instead, he would be seen as a man of faith and of purity.

The ABCs of Cleansing

- **Ask** God to cleanse you from the defilement of evil reports. Take a close look at the attitudes, comments and offenses in your life. As you go before God and present your life to Him, He will show you those areas of repentance that must take place. "I beseech you therefore, brethren, by the mercies of God, that you present your bodies a living sacrifice, holy, acceptable to God, which is your reasonable service" (Romans 12:1).

- **Be** diligent in prayer during this season. While there are many people who may have defiled you with their words, likewise, you may have defiled many with your words. Begin to pray for those people you have injured, even inadvertently, by putting stumbling blocks in their walks with God. Ask God to bless those who have injured you and to reveal His glory to them. The Bible says to "bless those who curse you, and pray for those who spitefully use you" (Luke 6:28).

- **Cleanse** your thoughts and your mind continually. Listen to worship music; keep the prayers of God on your lips;

refuse to speak evil of others. You will be tempted not only by others but by your own thought life; you must refrain from falling back into the old habits. Do not believe a report to be true because it sounds convincing. "The simple believes every word, but the prudent considers well his steps" (Proverbs 14:15).

- Deliver yourself from the hands of the enemy by speaking truth about others as well as yourself. Bless those around you, pouring love upon them in speech and action. Allow the goodness of God to be an active part of your life, regardless of whether you are shopping, working, driving or sitting in your home. The light of Christ should be evident in all situations. "Love suffers long and is kind; love does not envy; love does not parade itself, is not puffed up; does not behave rudely, does not seek its own, is not provoked, thinks no evil; does not rejoice in iniquity, but rejoices in the truth" (1 Corinthians 13:4–6).

- Examine your motives in life. Why do you say certain things? Why do you listen to certain people? Are you willing to repent before those you have injured by your words or actions? God may see what we deem permissible as defiling. Seek the counsel of others and pray for God's discernment. "All the ways of a man are pure in his own eyes, but the LORD weighs the spirits" (Proverbs 16:2).

The cleansing process is not always enjoyable to go through, but in the end it is soothing to the soul. May we all be able to stand before God and know that we received His guidance and wisdom when speaking about other people. God wants us to be in unity and to be one in spirit. When we refuse to be a part of false stories, evil comments and innuendos, God is able to pour blessings upon each one of us and our families. Encourage one another and speak in ways that edify the Body of Christ. "Behold, how good and how pleasant it is for brethren to dwell together in unity!" (Psalm 133:1).

EXAMINING THE HEART

1. Which step of the cleansing process seems most difficult to you? Might this be an area that you need to bring before God?

2. Are there people you need to begin to speak blessings over instead of curses?

3. Are you able to go before God and declare yourself pure of the defilement of evil reports? If not, take time to repent and declare His cleansing.

13

Words That Heal

But no man can tame the tongue. It is an unruly evil, full of deadly poison.

James 3:8

I first met Jackson when he was seven years old. His mother, Laura, was hoping to enroll him in the newly formed Big Brother/Big Sister program. As administrator of the program, I had the opportunity to interview Jackson and his mother. He certainly fit the profile for our program.

Laura's husband left her when Jackson was two years old. She recounted multiple instances of abuse, domestic violence and drug involvement by her husband. Confused in her victimization, she allowed much of the abuse to occur for fear of losing him. It was after Laura received a near-death beating and threats of the same toward Jackson that she finally sought help.

As soon as a restraining order was issued, Jackson's father left the state. Five years had passed and this young, withdrawn boy had not seen or heard from his father. Laura went back to school and got a job at a local grocery store as an assistant manager. They had only recently moved into the community and were seeking support systems. Laura spotted a newspaper advertisement for our program, and they came to the office to seek out more information.

As was often the case, we had many more requests for Brothers and Sisters than we had adults to fill the spots. But there was something about the way Jackson looked at me with his soft blue eyes. I could only imagine the fear and hurt he had suffered, yet there was an innocence about him. While there were no Big Brothers on the availability list, I knew this young boy had found a place in my heart. I became Jackson's Big Brother.

Over the next year Jackson and I got together at least once a week. We went fishing, played catch, took drives, rode bikes and generally enjoyed one another's company. It did not take long to see a gaping hole in his emotional framework. He regularly made negative comments about himself. "I'm stupid," "I hate myself" and "I wish I were dead" were common remarks. Having come from a home where my parents spoke love and encouragement, I found these declarations to be foreign. Why would someone say such things about himself? I did not understand.

What I did understand was that Jackson needed truth spoken to him. He needed someone to begin to break through his wall of self-protection. His feelings and fear of abandonment made it difficult to get close to him emotionally. It became my mission to destroy the "old tapes" within his mind and replace them with new thought processes. Each week I encouraged him, told him how smart he was and worked to build his self-esteem. For a long time it seemed to have little impact. Then, after six to seven months of pouring truth into his life, I saw a glimmer of hope.

Jackson turned to me one day and said, "Mike, my teacher says that I am really smart. Do you think I am?" For months I had been telling him this, so I knew he was expecting an affirmative answer. I realized, though, that what I thought was not nearly as critical as what he thought about himself. I responded in a way that surprised him. "Jackson," I said, "what do you think?"

He looked at me a bit suspiciously. Then he said, "I think I'm pretty smart, when I want to be." Hallelujah! A positive comment! I could hardly contain my joy. A kind word from a teacher, a word of encouragement from a friend, a statement of hope from a parent can give new life to a child's dreams.

We simply do not comprehend the power that our words have. Even thoughtless words that have no evil intent can have great power. When my son Jason was in the sixth grade, he was undergoing testing to determine learning styles. His teacher innocently, but ignorantly, told him that his aptitude was not in math. According to the test results, unless his teachers used special techniques, Jason would not do well in math. As parents and educators, my wife and I found that interesting since our son had never had problems with math before. We shrugged off the test results and the comments by the teacher.

Suddenly, though, Jason began to struggle in math. From that year on he found it a difficult subject, one that required extra hard work. Through high school and college, from pre-algebra to calculus, Jason battled a mental block concerning his ability to perform in standard ways without the help of special activities. If one comment by one person who had not intended to be demeaning could have such long-term ramifications, how devastating are intentional words of pain and cruelty? They are hard to overcome, but with enough encouragement and love it can happen.

For my Little Brother, Jackson, the positive approach of his teacher was just the beginning of his transformation. After a year or so Laura was transferred to another town and given a managerial position. Many tears were shed (not all by Jackson) as we prepared for their move. But before me stood an eight-year-old boy who had gained enough confidence to believe that he was going to make it in life. We exchanged letters regularly for the next few months, but after a year or two I lost contact with him. As I recall my experience with Jackson, I am amazed by the power of words to heal. God replaced Jackson's old patterns of self-hate and discouragement with love and hope.

Though Jesus' methods varied depending upon the situation and the people He was addressing, His words were intended for freedom, release, restoration and reconciliation. He spoke words of challenging truth to the Pharisees and religious leaders. He spoke words of enlightenment to the centurion, Nicodemus and Zacchaeus. He spoke words of deliverance to the thief on the cross, the leprous man and many who were demonized. He spoke words of healing to the Syrophoenician woman, to Mary Magdalene, to the woman at the well. What words do you speak to people? Are you an instrument of inspiration or a tool of torture? Do you build up or tear down? Is it easier to attack or to protect a person? Is your first reaction to get revenge or to restore a relationship? Do you bless or curse those around you?

Joseph's Words of Release

> Patience and gentle talk can convince a ruler and overcome any problem.
>
> Proverbs 25:15 CEV

There was a young man who was mocked by his family, laughed at, dealt with harshly and eventually totally rejected by those he loved. Yet later in life, when given an opportunity for revenge, he spoke words of kindness, healing and love to those who had wronged him. Let's look closer at the story of Joseph, found in Genesis 37–50.

Joseph was one of the sons of Jacob. Because Joseph was born late in Jacob's life, his father had a special affection for him. When Joseph was seventeen years old, he was given prophetic dreams from God. In them, he saw his older brothers, his father and his mother bowing down to him. When he told his family of his dreams, they were offended at the audacity of this boy to suggest he would be their leader. So incensed were his brothers by this "revelation" of his impending lordship over them, as well as by the favoritism shown Joseph by their father, they plotted to rid themselves of this troublesome boy. The motivation of the brothers could have been fear, jealousy or even the fact that they themselves, down deep, witnessed to the truth of the prophetic dreams.

They cast Joseph into a pit and eventually sold him into slavery. Imagine . . . seventeen years old, rejected by your family, sold into slavery and forced to survive in a foreign country. Joseph's temptation toward anger and bitterness must have been great. I wonder how many nights, while traveling on the road to Egypt, Joseph replayed the scene of his brothers' betrayal? But Joseph refused to succumb to feelings of isolation; he must have held on to the fact that God remained with him. Potiphar, the captain of the guard in Pharaoh's court, saw something special in Joseph. He bought him from the slave traders and showed him favor.

Soon, however, betrayal was again close at hand. Potiphar's wife desired to be intimate with Joseph, but he refused to dishonor his master or his master's wife. Enraged by this rejection, Potiphar's wife claimed that Joseph had attacked her and tried to rape her. Joseph was immediately arrested and thrown into the dungeon. Again Joseph had an opportunity for bitterness.

Yet even in the dungeons the anointing of God was again seen on Joseph, and he was given the responsibility of overseeing all the prisoners. The baker and the butler of the court had fallen into disfavor with Pharaoh and were condemned to prison. While in the dungeons of the king, they had dreams and were looking for an interpretation. Joseph, through godly insight, gave them the interpretation, asking only to be remembered if they were released from prison. Indeed, the chief butler was soon restored to his position, but he quickly forgot his promise to remember Joseph.

Think about it. Joseph had numerous times of hurt and disappointment. He had ample reason to be offended and to spread evil reports about his brothers, Potiphar and the butler. Yet during all the accounts of Joseph, we read only of a faithful man. I believe it is safe to say that if he had allowed anger, frustration or bitterness to rule his spirit, he would not have maintained God's anointing.

As is often the way of God with those who are faithful to Him, Joseph was given an opportunity to speak truth to a person of great influence: Pharaoh himself. Joseph was asked to interpret his dreams, and as he did so, Pharaoh saw the authority of God on his life.

> And Pharaoh said to his servants, "Can we find such a one as this, a man in whom is the Spirit of God?" Then Pharaoh said to Joseph, "Inasmuch as God has shown you all this, there is no one as discerning and wise as you. You shall be over my house and all my people shall be ruled according to your word; only in regard to the throne will I be greater than you."
>
> Genesis 41:38–40

Joseph was now a man of power. The lonely, isolated, rejected boy had risen to a position of influence and authority. Yet in the back of his mind he still remembered his family. He secretly longed for the opportunity to see them, to speak to them. But the plan of God is always miraculous and beyond our understanding.

During this time there was a famine in the land. Through godly insight, Joseph had, for many years, been storing food so the people of the region would survive the years of famine. His brothers went to Egypt to obtain food for the family. Joseph recognized his brothers, but he had changed so much they did not know him.

Genesis 45 is the powerful account of Joseph's revealing his true identity to his family. Here was the moment for revenge. The opportunity to get back at the brothers for their treachery was now at hand. Joseph could finally exact retribution for the years of suffering and betrayal. However, in one glorious moment, with one powerful statement, Joseph spoke healing words upon his family and attempted to put to death forever the bondage of guilt within his brothers: "Do not therefore be grieved or angry with yourselves because you sold me here; for God sent me before you to preserve life. . . . So it was not you who sent me here, but God" (Genesis 45:5, 8). Though Joseph tried to impart freedom to his brothers, the chains of fear held them tightly.

Let me mention here that it is important to continue to speak assurance to people during times of fear and uncertainty. In order to heal with words, we must be willing to be persistent with them. Jesus frequently verbalized His love for His disciples. Once is not enough! Encouragement, praise and positive words continue to feed the soul in the same way water moistens the soil. Soil will eventually dry out and need another dose of fresh water.

As a husband, I have learned the importance of verbally stating "I love you" to my wife. Early in our marriage I thought to myself, *I told her I loved her yesterday. I told her last week. I told her the day we were married. Why does she want me to say those words so often?* While my love and faithfulness for my wife were not in doubt, some of her previous experiences had opened doors of pain and fear. In order to break those chains of despair, I needed to be consistent in speaking truth to her. Over the years, my words of love have been instrumental in God's process of healing in her.

Thus it was with Joseph. The day came that his father, Jacob, died and his brothers were left with a sense of fear and dread. "What if he now wants to kill us?" "Did he only keep us alive because of our father?" Again Joseph spoke healing, compassionate words to his brothers—words that finally released them from bondage.

> "Do not be afraid, for am I in the place of God? But as for you, you meant evil against me; but God meant it for good, in order to bring it about as it is this day, to save many people alive. Now therefore, do not be afraid; I will provide for you and your little ones." And he comforted them and spoke kindly to them.
>
> Genesis 50:19–21

With these words, peace washed over their hearts. Joseph was a man who used his words to heal his brothers.

God's Words of Encouragement

The story of Joseph is one biblical example of many in which words were used to bring freedom and healing. I want to give two other examples. In these instances it was God who did the speaking. He looked past flaws and called forth true character. Let's look briefly at the words God spoke to Gideon and Moses.

Gideon was threshing wheat in a winepress in order to hide it from the marauding Midianites. While this may have been a smart thing to do, it was an unusual place to find the next judge of Israel. "And the Angel of the LORD appeared to him, and said to him, 'The LORD is with you, you mighty man of valor!'" (Judges 6:12). Does it seem odd to you that the Angel called a man hiding in a winepress "a mighty man of valor"? Gideon's reaction might seem odder still: Gideon began arguing with the Angel of the Lord. Let's think about this! We have here not the sweetly smiling television show variety of angel. This was the Angel of the Lord and Gideon argued, disagreed and generally complained about the way God was treating the Israelites.

Upon Gideon's completion of his monologue of whines and complaints, we see an astonishing transition. Gideon had been talking with the Angel about the Lord's dealings with Israel, but now we read that "the LORD turned to him." From this point on Gideon addressed the Lord directly, though still complaining. And amazingly, the Lord spoke words of encouragement to him: "Go in this might of yours, and you shall save Israel from the hand of the Midianites. Have I not sent you?" (Judges 6:14). Although Gideon had questioned the plans of God and called himself the least in his father's house, the Lord was faithful to speak words of healing and strength to Gideon's purpose and destiny in life.

This was the same pattern when Moses was confronted by the image of God in the burning bush. God spoke clearly to Moses with words of direction and hope, but Moses responded with doubt, disbelief and discouragement. "But suppose they will not believe me or listen to my voice; suppose they say 'The LORD has not appeared to you'" (Exodus 4:1). "O my LORD, I am not eloquent, neither before nor since You have spoken to Your servant; but I am slow of speech and slow of tongue" (Exodus 4:10). "Who am I that I should go to Pharaoh, and that I should bring the children of Israel out of Egypt?" (Exodus 3:11). While we often see ourselves as inept and unable, God sees beyond our excuses and into the realm of possibilities in Him, and He speaks the words that will encourage and direct us.

Our Choices of Words

I have heard it said that for every negative word we speak toward a person, it takes up to ten positive words to counteract those previous words. While never testing this scientifically, I experienced it in a way that I have never forgotten. It was after I spoke at a seminar with more than a hundred participants. They were asked to complete an evaluation of the seminar and a compilation of the comments was sent to me. As my wife and I began to go through the evaluations, we found them overwhelmingly positive. One of them, however, was not. The participant found my presentation less than inspiring, containing "basic information and lacking in a theoretical framework."

After we read through all of the comments, Joyce was cheery and excited. I, on the other hand, felt discouraged and lackluster. As we talked further, it became apparent that one evaluation had taken center stage to all the others. The negative feedback of one review had effectively crushed the encouragement of more than one hundred people. What a lesson in the power of negative words! I still take all feedback, positive or negative, very seriously, but I no longer give a greater weight to the critic than I do the encourager.

Great people of God find a way to speak hope into others. They give a sense of purpose, of calling, of future, of destiny to those around them. From Moses to Daniel, from Abraham Lincoln to Martin Luther King Jr., each spoke words that brought change to many lives. Winston Churchill spoke words of promise over his country. Adolf Hitler spoke words of pain and death over his. Abraham instilled hope and future blessings over his children. King Saul spoke curses and hatred over his. The challenge before each of us is whether we will build a life with words of healing or destroy a life with words of criticism.

God wants to build up. Negative words tear down. As Christians we are called to share with others about Christ's message of love. Let's watch our words carefully, but more important, let's all begin to speak active words of healing.

═══ EXAMINING THE HEART ═══

1. Keep track of your comments to someone who looks up to you (your children, younger siblings, a new young employee) for one hour. Are your comments positive, building the person up? Even if your words of guidance and correction are positive, what about your tone and inflection?

2. Do you attempt to speak healing words as Joseph did? Over the next week be cognizant of your words. Speak words that heal.

14

Restoring Relationships

As we look back at the importance of carefully choosing our words, as well as filtering out the negative conversations to which we are exposed, we must also address the problem of how to restore broken relationships. What if my words caused such damage that my friend, my sibling or my parent no longer trusts me? What if my unkind words and runaway conversations have effectively severed my relationships with the people I care about?

On the other hand, how should I respond to others when I have been wounded by their words? Is there a way to bring healing to a broken and damaged friendship and relationship?

Our lives may be littered with painful memories of how we treated people and, at times, how others treated us. In many cases, we would have liked to bridge the chasm between us but were uncertain as to how to proceed. In this chapter, I want to lay out a clear course of action, one that will assist us to rebuild those broken connections. Will the course of action I am proposing be foolproof? Will it work every time? Because we can only control what we ourselves do, the answer is, of course not. However, no matter how the other person reacts, we can control our own attitude to their reaction.

Looking in the Mirror

King David found himself separated from God because of incredibly poor choices, including lying, adultery and, oh yeah, murder! David ordered Bathsheba to his home and slept with her while her husband was away at war. She became pregnant. David then sent Uriah to certain death in battle so David could marry Bathsheba. He refused to repent or acknowledge his sin for nearly a year. Finally, Nathan the prophet challenged David and encouraged him to find a place of repentance and brokenness.

In Psalm 51:10–12, David, desperate to restore his broken relationship with God, appeals to Him:

> Create in me a clean heart, O God, and renew a steadfast spirit within me. Do not cast me away from Your presence, and do not take Your Holy Spirit from me. Restore to me the joy of Your salvation and uphold me by Your generous Spirit.

David longs to heal the gap between himself and God. He focuses on his own transgressions and humbles himself before God. In Psalm 51, we find a solid recipe for reconciliation. The ingredients include humility, personal responsibility, honesty, accountability and a desire to change.

Barriers to Restoring Relationships

> One lie has the power to tarnish a thousand truths.
>
> Al David, author

Harsh words between a loving husband and wife can fester for hours, even days. Words spoken in frustration toward a child may cause a rift for weeks, even months. Thoughtless comments to a relative or friend have the power to damage that relationship forever. What is it about our words that cut so deeply that we find it difficult to recover from their wounds?

We can replay words of criticism, judgment and negativity over and over again, resurrecting wounds and scars even years after the original altercation. Although we may have wanted to reconcile initially, or even over time, what had once been a fissure in our relationship seems to have grown into a veritable ravine filled with thorny brambles and bushes. Any venture into that ravine, no matter how well-intentioned, seems fraught with danger.

Several key factors come into play when we look at the possible barriers to moving toward reconciliation and restoration of relationships.

A wounded spirit (or emotional hurt)

To illustrate the first barrier, let us consider the story of Robert, a gregarious and fun-loving person, louder than most people—his laughter may be heard across a room. Robert loves to talk, loves to joke with others, but he is also adamant about his perspective and, as a result, tends to be insensitive to others' feelings. He enjoys a good debate and often pushes a conversation beyond what is comfortable for those around him. His tendency to do so resulted in placing a wedge between him and a fellow employee.

Over the course of many weeks, Robert teased and goaded a colleague about a mistake she had made during a meeting. At first, the teasing was good-natured and she thought of it as just "Robert being Robert." When he persisted, his teasing became tiresome, even embarrassing to her. When she asked him to stop, Robert said, "Can't you take a joke?"

Her inability to laugh off what he considered his "good-natured" chiding only fueled Robert's efforts to prolong the joke.

Finally, she complained to their supervisor, who, in turn, sat down with Robert. The supervisor, not a close friend to Robert but someone who socialized with him occasionally, attempted to understand Robert's point of view.

Robert felt attacked. He resented being "called on the carpet" for what he considered "a little good-natured fun." The supervisor, realizing that he was not getting anywhere, asked Robert to meet again in a few days, hoping that by the time they met again, Robert would have cooled down and would not feel so attacked. Unfortunately, the subsequent meeting went even worse. Robert swore at him, and in the heat of the moment, he walked out, quitting his job. In the days that followed, Robert rebuffed all attempts by his supervisor to reconnect.

Several months went by, and even though they lived in the same community, the supervisor and Robert did not cross paths. However, the supervisor heard that Robert was unrepentant, even rude when he did run into former co-workers. Robert's perspective of the situation was negative toward the co-worker, the supervisor and the company. Critical comments were at the forefront of many of his conversations.

One night at a local sporting event, the supervisor saw Robert. Although Robert acknowledged him with only a perfunctory nod, the supervisor felt the need to reach out to him. So a few days later he stopped by Robert's house. He asked for forgiveness, explaining that he had not meant to be harsh or insensitive. He attempted to explain the awkward position he had been in—having to support the offended colleague while attempting to understand Robert's position. Their talk, though cordial, elicited no deep understanding or receptiveness from

Robert, and the supervisor left feeling that he had done all that he could, and that the stories about Robert and his attitude had, obviously, been accurate.

It was a year or so later that I received a letter from Robert. (Yes, in case you have not figured it out, I was the supervisor.) I will paraphrase and summarize his comments.

He asked for my forgiveness for not receiving my gesture of reconciliation. He told me that after I visited him, his wife and he had many conversations. As a result, Robert realized that after he quit work, he felt ignored, even shunned by his friends and colleagues. He blamed everyone else for the consequences of his actions and their resulting pain. Then he made a statement that made me evaluate my own heart and attitude. He said, "I ask for your forgiveness for my words and actions. However, if you can't forgive me, that is up to you. The ball is in your court. All I can do is reach out and share how God has shown me my own culpability in the situation. I feel free now."

Robert was right. All he could do was reach out, share his heart and ask for forgiveness. We can learn from him. If we reach out, share our heart and ask for forgiveness, we should feel released from guilt and condemnation. I appreciated Robert's words and took them to heart. I investigated my own willingness (or unwillingness) to reconcile with Robert. I wrote back to offer my own forgiveness and appreciation for his letter. Since then, he and I have connected several times and have forged a comfortable relationship with one another.

A wounded spirit may cause us to feel rejected and isolated. It may distort our perception of reality, or at least magnify the actual events. As with Robert (and with King David), the event can be so painful that it becomes easier to ignore than to confront. Of course, it would be presumptuous to compare the situation between Robert and me to the situation that existed between King David and the prophet Nathan! The only similarity is that in our situation, I was willing to take the time to communicate truth and love to Robert, and although my efforts were certainly not received with open arms, they helped open communication between Robert and his wife. Sometimes, reaching out to the offended person allows him or her to begin to evaluate and formulate a new perspective.

For my part, I came to see that an evil report had definitely skewed my perspective and sensitivity to Robert. I realized that I had allowed other people's perceptions of Robert to influence me even before he and I had that fateful meeting. Because of that evil report, I had not begun that meeting unprejudiced and impartial as I, the supervisor, should have been. Even more significant, as a Christian, I want my words to be supportive and encouraging and to bring others toward a place of peace and healing, not inject pain into their lives.

People who have been hurt need support and compassion. They may also need time to process and to find a way to communicate and interact positively. We must be willing to walk through that process with them. I stopped short of pursuing Robert for reconciliation. I became impatient and upset at his unwillingness to change. I had my own time frame. He had not managed to work out his pain and anger within that time frame, and as the clock I had set for him ran out, I washed my hands of him. I had "taken the high road," and he did not meet me there, and that was that. Fortunately, Robert had a patient wife and a God of grace and mercy who allowed him to work through his pain on his own terms, in a much more generous time frame.

An unwillingness to accept personal responsibility

Throughout 1 Samuel, we read about King Saul's attitude toward David. He was jealous of David's success and notoriety among the people. King Saul felt threatened by David and was fearful that he would usurp his authority and his throne.

> Thus Saul saw and knew that the Lord was with David, and that Michal, Saul's daughter, loved him; and Saul was still more afraid of David. So Saul became David's enemy continually.
>
> 1 Samuel 18:28–29

David's early life is filled with encounters with a raging Saul who blamed David for his lack of popularity, his mistakes in life and the loss of relationship with his son Jonathan.

In Saul's mind, David was the bad guy. Saul would be satisfied with nothing short of David's leaving the kingdom or, perhaps, David's death. David eventually went into hiding to avoid confrontations with Saul and to preserve his own life. There was nothing David could say or do that would appease Saul. King Saul refused to accept responsibility for his part in the relationship between himself and David. Saul's refusal to accept that he was part of the problem put up a wall between them that could not be breached.

Unfortunately, as is common in these situations, Saul became bitter. He lost his faith in God, moved toward worshiping idols and engaging in witchcraft and lost the support of loved ones. If we are not able to look in the mirror and accept our personal responsibility, we may become frustrated, even angry at those around us.

Fear

This fear may be of reprisal, of change, of trusting again. We find this issue illustrated in the story of Joseph. We know that Joseph's brothers sold him into slavery and that in time Joseph was elevated to a position that allowed him to bless his own family. Although Joseph opened his heart and kingdom to his brothers, they feared retaliation. As a result, they lied to him about their father's final words.

> When Joseph's brothers saw that their father was dead, they said, "Perhaps Joseph will hate us, and may actually repay us for all the evil which we did to him." So they sent messengers to Joseph, saying "Before your father died he commanded, saying, 'Thus you shall say to Joseph, "I beg you, please forgive the trespass of your brothers and their sin."'"
>
> Genesis 50:15–17

Joseph responded with compassion and brokenness, weeping as he heard these words. Fear had kept his family bound and prevented them from fully embracing the love Joseph had for them. Instead of feeling relieved and free by Joseph's kind and compassionate gestures, his brothers lived in the bondage of fear.

Gossip and negative conversation influenced an entire family. Perhaps the instigator of that fearful thinking was just one brother, but whatever the case, it infected all of them, resulting in lies and deception toward their own brother. How unfortunate that his family was unable to fully enjoy the joy of restoration.

The power of forgiveness breaks through barriers and opens up doors to allow reconciliation and restoration. David and Joseph understood the power of forgiveness, and they had the mercy and grace to extend it to those around them. Jesus wants us to do the same.

The Heart of Restoration

Our own pain, our refusal to accept personal responsibility for our part in the problem and our fear prevent us from allowing true reconciliation to occur. But is there a way we can work through these barriers? Can we follow a process that will increase the likelihood of successful restoration of relationship?

> Moreover if your brother sins against you, go and tell him his fault between you and him alone. If he hears you, you have gained your brother. But if he will not hear, take with you one or two more, that "by the mouth of two or three witnesses every word may be established." And if he refuses to hear them, tell it to the church. But if he refuses even to hear the church, let him be to you like a heathen or tax collector.
>
> Matthew 18:15–17

This is a guideline for restoring a person who has fallen into a sinful pattern or behavior. It also explains how we should approach someone who has offended us. Let's be honest. When we have a broken relationship with someone, our attitude is usually that the other person has done something wrong, that they have committed a type of sin. That sin could be lying, cruelty or perhaps gossip, to name just a few. Most relationships are not broken simply because we have a mild disagreement and "agree to disagree." Relationships break because we are hurt, wounded, angered, etc. We believe the other party needs to be properly chastised and punished.

We need, however, to be willing to let go of those feelings and allow God's love and grace to move in our lives. Restoration and reconciliation must be the banner we raise in our lives instead of allowing anger and bitterness to grow within us.

Let's evaluate Matthew 18:15–17 line by line.

"If your brother sins against [offends] you, go and tell him his fault between you and him alone. If he hears you, you have gained your brother." How often should we go to this person? I often need to hear someone's explanation and ideas more than once to truly grasp their significance. In response to a question from Peter, Jesus tells us how many times we are to forgive a person who has offended us or sinned against us. "Jesus said to him, 'I do not say to you, up to seven times, but up to seventy times seven'" (verse 22).

Did Jesus really mean 490 times? I certainly have never been that tenacious in approaching anyone or in offering my forgiveness! Numbers aside, suffice it to say, we should go to the person numerous times in an effort to win them over and to attempt reconciliation and a restoration of relationship.

Jesus approached His disciples countless times in order to explain parables and life situations. He continually discussed proverbs and guidelines. Over and over, He encouraged the masses toward faith, conviction and understanding. Though frustrated at times by their inability to clearly hear His message and by their unwillingness to grasp the truth of His words, He was faithful to continue to approach them in hopes of reconciling them to the Father.

"But if he will not hear, take with you one or two more, that 'by the mouth of two or three witnesses every word may be established.'" This is an important area to examine. The counsel is to take other people with you as witnesses. Let's start with the word *witness*. What is a witness? Someone who sees something, who can testify as to what occurred, correct? That means it is not necessarily someone who agrees with you or someone you choose because he or she will support you. A witness, by definition, watches, observes and then gives feedback as to what actually occurs.

It is human nature in such situations to choose just the right person to go with us, a kindred spirit who will take our side and support our approach. The result is that the person we are trying to help feels "ganged up on," attacked and mistrustful. To ensure that will not be the case, find a person he or she also feels comfortable with as your witness. Explain what is expected of the witness, and then ask that witness to give both of you feedback as to how well you are both listening, how clearly you are communicating and if you are both honestly working toward restoration. The witness's job is to keep you both accountable. If that is the case, the conversation will go much more smoothly, be laced with less emotion and, hopefully, achieve the intended result.

Parents, you might consider using this method with your children. Instead of rushing to solve the problem between Jimmy and Sarah, take on the role of a witness.

Jimmy: "Mommy (or Daddy), Sarah is calling me names and won't stop."

Parent: "Have you asked her to stop?"

Jimmy: "Yes, but she won't listen."

Parent: "Okay, let me come with you." (Once with both children, turn to Jimmy.) "Go ahead, Jimmy. Ask again, and I will watch."

Such an interaction teaches your children the social skill of working through their own problems with effective communication. Do not jump in to rescue the child; allow them to communicate with each other, and you as the witness give feedback along the way.

You will also find that in many situations, the name-caller or bully or unkind party will stop his or her negative behavior simply because of your presence. Yet still, the child feeling victimized will be empowered by communicating his or her personal needs.

"And if he refuses to hear them, tell it to the church." I find this part of the process to be the most confusing and potentially harmful part of the restoration process. "Tell it to the church." Hmm. Who, exactly, are we calling the church? Is it the Body of Christ at large? Is it the local congregation? Is it the elders? We need to figure that out before we begin the process.

I have seen issues brought before a church on a Sunday morning and I have cringed! After all, in a Sunday service, who is in attendance? Only members? Only believers? Certainly not! Then why are we parading our issues in front of people who might have no idea about godly reconciliation and who certainly have no need to hear them? This type of gossip and criticism only serves to alienate people and push them further away from God. What was the motive of the person taking it to the church? Shame? Defamation? Embarrassment? Shaming someone into repentance? God help us! I believe that is not at all what God intended when he asked us to tell it to the church.

God wants restoration of relationships. If we are told to take it to the church, the point is to reconcile the person with others and with God. So before we air someone else's dirty laundry on a Sunday morning, we had better think about the purpose and motives of our actions. Most people will not get "embarrassed" back into relationship. And if they can, that relationship will be short-lived.

It has been my experience that the "church" might be local leadership or elders in the church. It might be a group of accountability partners who care and cherish their brother or sister. I believe God intended to bring our concerns before people who have such a heart of love and compassion for the person being confronted, people who will be moved toward prayer and action on behalf of that person—an intervention approach, if you will.

Throughout the letters of Paul, we find him referencing people who need help and prayer. He was not gossiping or using negativity to injure these people. His intent was not to share their issues with everyone, but to a select few who loved and cherished each individual. Remember, Paul sent personal letters. His intention was to activate the Body of Christ in order to redeem an individual.

Let nothing be done through selfish ambition or conceit, but in lowliness of mind let each esteem others better than himself. Let each of you look out not only for his own interests, but also for the interests of others.

Philippians 2:3–4

And when two people were bickering and causing division in the church, he requested people to assist the two in reconciling.

I implore Euodia and I implore Syntyche to be of the same mind in the Lord. And I urge you also, true companion, help these women who labored with me in the gospel.

Philippians 4:2–3

Paul's heart was not to be critical or negative toward these people. He wanted to set up a plan for restoration in their lives.

"But if he refuses even to hear the church, let him be to you like a heathen or tax collector." This last command is often interpreted by churches as synonymous with excommunicating or shunning. Is that really what God intends for His people? If God is really saying, "If they won't listen, never talk to them again," who will speak truth to them? If no one reaches out in love, how can our brothers and sisters ever come to a place of reconciliation? Isn't turning our back on someone the opposite of grace?

I am so grateful that in all my hardheadedness and lack of responsiveness to God's efforts in my life, He never cut me off. The door was always open. A bridge is always available for me to walk across to find freedom.

How did Jesus treat sinners, heathens and tax collectors? Did he ignore them, hate them, shun them? No! He ate with them, communed with them, spoke truth to them! Remember, that is one reason the Pharisees were so upset with Jesus. He ate with sinners and tax collectors! (See Luke 5:30.)

Please do not interpret my statements as license to hang out with whomever you want and do whatever you want under the banner of "grace." I am not condoning being involved in illegal or immoral activities under the guise of winning over the lost. We are called to take a stand for who we are in Christ, while being open to communicating with those who are lost.

We are called to move in love, compassion and grace toward reconciling people. Once we have moved faithfully through the directions for reconciliation God has laid out, we may not become "best friends." But are we praying for them, speaking kindly of them? Are we willing to reach out to them and to speak truth into their lives? Our interactions may not be about sporting events, our families or what we did over the weekend. Instead, our discussions will be filled with guidance, God's truth and love and an open heart to receive the offender back into God's will. We reach out to them, not to agree with their attitudes or actions but to help them see God's mercy and plan for their lives.

Restoration and reconciliation are at the heart of God's plan. He chose to send His Son to die for our transgressions so we could be reconciled to the Father. Two thousand years of history have not changed the heart of God. He still wants us reconciled to Him and to one another. Without a willingness to show forgiveness and grace, relationships will remain fractured and broken.

═══ EXAMINING THE HEART ═══

1. Is God bringing to mind someone you have stopped praying for or reaching out to?

2. What can you do to start the reconciliation process with that person? Reread Matthew 18. Allow God to speak to you regarding His heart of restoration.

15

Closer to Home

Kirk and Amber are a devoted couple with three beautiful children. They have had a few rocky moments in their marriage, but through counseling, marriage seminars and drawing closer to God, they have been able to overcome many obstacles. Unfortunately, one area that they have been unable to conquer is the tendency to be offended. When this happens, their lips speak words of negativity toward anyone who will listen.

There was the time, for instance, when Amber felt that other children in the church were mistreating her five-year-old daughter. She telephoned one of the pastors and spoke harshly and critically toward a number of children, saying that they had called her daughter names and pushed her down. Amber then proceeded to call a number of people and pass on her frustration. Finally, after a series of meetings, Amber and Kirk realized they had misunderstood the situation: Their child had pushed another child first, then retaliation had occurred. After they saw the complete picture, they apologized to the pastor and continued with their previous support of him and the general direction of the church.

About two weeks after the first incident, Kirk and Amber's older teenager told this to a high school youth leader: "My dad and mom don't think you do a good job caring about us. They say you don't watch us very closely when we are in our meetings." It was no more than a day or two later that another altercation took place with their five-year-old. This time the little girl turned to the Sunday school teacher and said, "My parents said I don't have to come if you are going to let the kids beat me up." Both the youth leader and Sunday school teacher were at a loss as to what to say or do. The parents appeared to be undermining the authority and respect of the leaders yet were not discussing it with them directly.

It was during our annual teen camp retreat that Kirk and Amber began to see the fruit of their defilement. Approximately 250 teenagers from within a network of churches were in attendance. Kirk and Amber's two teenagers did not want to attend. Not only did the children speak angrily and bitterly about the leaders and other members of the youth group, but they argued with their parents about whether or not God was real and whether or not going to church was really that important. Kirk and Amber were beside themselves, asking for intervention, prayer and encouragement as their children seemed to be slipping away. They wanted their children to be a part of the camp, to attend church and to grow closer to God. They remained oblivious to the poisonous words they had spoken in recent months and the impact they had had on their family.

In this book we have looked at the many tracks that evil reports ride toward deception. We have seen the impact on the lives of those who gossip and murmur and those who listen.

And we have seen that cleansing is possible. Generally, we have viewed this topic as it affects us currently—that is, as we seek forgiveness, restoration and freedom in the difficult situations we face daily. In this final chapter, let us take a moment to address how these evil reports will affect the future, the next generation. Most of us have some impact on the lives of children, whether as parents, Sunday school teachers, aunts and uncles, Girl Scout leaders, Big Brothers or even baby-sitters. These children are our next generation, and the lessons we teach them are the lessons they will teach their children.

What conversations occur at *your* dinner table with young people present? Are the words you speak in your home supportive of authority and leadership, or do you give subtle impressions that you find it objectionable? How do you speak about your supervisors, your friends, your spouse—all within earshot of little listening ears? Defilement is passed on from one person to another and from one generation to the next.

Look around and you will likely see this in action. It is not hard to find, for instance, students who hide behind their parents' anger and frustration toward their schools. These parents might be transmitting feelings born out of their own negative experiences: "So what if my child isn't doing well in history. I didn't do well either and I made it." As adults, our personal perspectives carry tremendous weight in the eyes of youth. Do not believe the lie that says the younger generation does not listen to older people. That is false. They listen, they watch and they make judgments based on an adult's character and integrity in a situation. What behavior are you showing to the children in your life? Are you a comforter or a complainer? A worshiper or a whiner? A prayer warrior or a self-centered whimperer?

I recently read this story by Billy Graham about the ramifications of gossip:

There is a story of a woman in England who came to her vicar with a troubled conscience. The vicar knew her to be a habitual gossip—she maligned nearly everyone in the village.

"How can I make amends?" she pleaded.

The vicar said, "If you want to make peace with your conscience, take a bag of goose feathers and drop one on the porch of each one you have slandered."

When she had done so, she came back to the vicar and said, "Is that all?"

"No," said the wise old minister, "you must go now and gather up every feather and bring them all back to me." After a long time the woman returned without a single feather. "The wind has blown them all away," she said.

"My good woman," said the vicar, "so it is with gossip. Unkind words are easily dropped, but we can never take them back again."

Are you speaking words that you would like to retrieve? What are you modeling to those around you?

I Should Know Better

It was the first day of school and our teenage son Aaron came home talking about his classes. Math, history, business . . . the usual list of classes for a junior in high school. All seemed fine until he mentioned his English class. Aaron had enrolled in an advanced English class even though in the previous year he was in a regular English class. We had not thought anything of it, as Aaron gets good grades and enjoys school. "English is a bummer," he said. "Last year the teacher assigned a book for the students to read over the summer. But I wasn't in her class last year. I didn't know about it and now I have two weeks to read this six-hundred-page book. Then I have to write a report and take a test." My wife and I looked at each other, our eyes saying, *The* other kids *had all summer to read the book but* our son *has only two weeks!* Without thinking I blurted out my thoughts: "Your teacher isn't being very fair. If you don't want to stay in that class, Aaron, we can get your schedule changed."

Here I was, in the midst of writing a book about evil reports and giving myself new material. Fortunately my son had been taught a stronger foundation. He replied, "No, I'll stay. It will just mean a lot of work for the next couple of weeks." I was embarrassed by my reaction to the situation. I almost caused my son to stumble due to my own lack of discipline with my tongue. I was sowing into his spirit seeds of disrespect and doubt about his teacher's wisdom and skill. Over the next week or so, when we talked about Aaron's schedule with other parents, they all spoke highly of his English teacher, saying how much he was going to love her class. I have since apologized to my son and explained the danger of what I said to him. Our homes can be breeding grounds for purity or pollution.

Children will test our spirits and reactions to situations. If they are challenged by one of life's struggles, they may look for us to ally ourselves with them. Do we rescue by consoling them without pursuing God's intentions for the matter? Too often we come to their defense at the expense of a teacher, a youth pastor, a boss or another child. I am not advocating ignoring our children or letting them suffer emotionally. But as hard as it is to imagine, my (or your) child might be wrong. He may have embellished a situation to benefit himself. Do we rush to defend our children, only to find out later that they were the ones who should be apologizing?

Prevention Guidelines

The following guidelines may help you prevent deception from creeping into your home or your relationship with a young person.

They may also help prevent you from being the one who spreads it. While they address the home, they are applicable to any situation in which you are in authority or leadership over children.

1. Guard the door of your house. If you hear people speaking false reports in your home, take authority over the situation. Speak out boldly: "I'd rather we not talk about someone who isn't here." If one of your children's friends is giving an evil report, interrupt him or her and set the boundaries. Your home should be a haven of peace and godliness; it is your place to guide and direct those placed within your care. "He who keeps instruction is in the way of life" (Proverbs 10:17).

2. Be accountable for your own speech. If you have spoken evil of another, there is no justification or rationale that will support you biblically. Speak clearly with your words and take responsibility for your actions. Marriage partners should hold each other accountable for purity in their speech. Ask your spouse to help you discipline your speech patterns. Allow your children to point out any time that you are giving an evil report. And as sons and daughters, allow your parents to challenge your speech habits in an effort to bring freedom to your life. No one likes to have his character destroyed by harsh words. We must pour out to others what we would like back in return. Remember the Golden Rule: "Therefore, whatever you want men to do to you, do also to them, for this is the Law and the Prophets" (Matthew 7:12).

3. Set up ground rules with your children. Be sure to include your children in the accountability area. How do they talk about their friends? Take one day and have each family member keep track of how many defiling comments are made by the family. Have a reward at the end of the day for all who are maturing in spiritual discipline. If you find that the tongue is out of control, have a "repentance party." Play worship music and pray for one another, drawing closer in your commitment to purity.

4. Check for poison in the house. How many times have you questioned your minister in a way that creates disunity and disharmony in the Body of Christ? Have you spoken negatively about your children's teachers, coaches or community leaders? When your children feel challenged by the youth pastor, have you supported this as a time of growth or undermined the suggestions? Sit down with your family and discuss attitudes toward leaders, friends and authorities in life. Do the children respect the adults and vice versa? Latent poison will eventually spread, and when it does it will contaminate all within its boundaries.

> Pursue peace with all people, and holiness, without which no one will see the Lord: looking carefully lest anyone fall short of the grace of God; lest any root of bitterness springing up cause trouble, and by this many become defiled.
>
> Hebrews 12:14–15

5. Examine your attitude and change it. We do not have to agree with everyone all the time. Of course, we will have differences of opinion, different ways of seeing things. We must, however, find a place of unity in God. I remember hearing this analogy: Four people were looking at a house. One was on the east side, one on the west side, one on the south side and one on the north side. When asked to describe the house, they all had different descriptions. Independently they were not in agreement, yet the descriptions, when put together, completed a picture of the house. Each one was correct, but no one picture was complete without the others.

6. Repent, repent, repent. If you have undermined or defiled another person, you must come to the Lord with a contrite heart. "A broken and contrite heart—these, O God, You will not despise" (Psalm 51:17). You may also find it necessary to go directly to the person and ask for forgiveness. The Jewish religion has a High Holy Day called Yom Kippur, which means Day of Atonement. On this day each year, Jews gather in synagogues across the world to repent of their sins. If they have sinned against God, they ask for His forgiveness. If they have sinned against another person, they seek that person out and ask for forgiveness. For Christians, every day is our "day of atonement." If we sin against man, we sin against God. Be honest in areas you need to atone for regarding defiling speech. Be cleansed by repenting and speaking cleansing words over others.

7. **Utilize the antidote for poison: love.** This is the antidote we have been given by our Savior. God is love. We need to combat our anger and bitterness with love.

> A new commandment I give to you, that you love one another; as I have loved you, that you also love one another. By this all will know that you are My disciples, if you have love for one another.
>
> John 13:34–35

May we all desire to be true disciples who speak love and encouragement to others.

8. **Teach your children, your church and your friends the process found in Matthew 18.** Help your children to understand reconciliation and restoration as described in the previous chapter. Over the years, I have spoken to many schools, especially middle schools, about this process. Most of the schools were secular, but I was able to teach the fundamental concepts communication, honesty, love and respect. The feedback I get from schools is one of excitement and appreciation as the students begin to work out their own problems and desire to reconcile with friends and family.

If we follow the above eight guidelines, our homes should have a sweeter aroma and our children should be kept safe from the defilement of evil reports.

Which Way Will We Go?

There are tracks that lead to deception and there is a pathway that leads to righteousness. I would like to conclude with two final stories from the Bible that encapsulate two distinctly different reactions to evil reports.

Jonathan's Honorable Stand

One of the most tragic examples of parenting is the story of King Saul trying to defile his son Jonathan. As I described in earlier chapters, Saul constantly spoke polluting stories about David. He cursed David, told lies about him and did everything in his power to destroy David's reputation and his life. Through it all, however, Jonathan refused to be defiled. He held fast to the biblical principle of not being a false witness, thus refusing to be used as his father's weapon by speaking bitter words. "Hide me from the secret plots of the wicked . . . who sharpen their tongue like a sword, and bend their bows to shoot their arrows—bitter words" (Psalm 64:2–3). Jonathan was an exceptionally strong spiritual person. Most of us would succumb (and have) to this type of barrage, but not Jonathan. He had made a covenant with David to be honest and true to his friend. Jonathan refused to let an evil report tarnish his perspective of the person to whom he was committed.

Absalom's Defiled Life

Earlier in this book we also discussed Absalom, his separation from his father, David, and the memorial he built to himself at the end of his life, saying, "I have no son to keep my name in remembrance" (2 Samuel 18:18). Poor Absalom! He was all alone, no vision of the future that could carry his name forward. But is that accurate? Was Absalom without family?

In 2 Samuel 14:27 we find an interesting piece of information: "To Absalom were born three sons, and one daughter whose name was Tamar." Indeed, Absalom had sons, and he had a daughter whom he named after his sister. Why would Absalom say later in life he had no sons? Could it be that he created a division between himself and his children by his bitter and evil reports? Were they so estranged in relationship that he disowned them (or they disowned him)? Although we cannot be totally sure what occurred, it is safe to say that Absalom's defiled spirit created such dissension in his own family that he was left alone in the latter stages of his life.

On any given day, we may be confronted by careless words coming from friends or strangers. Some words are directed toward us, and others we just happen to overhear. Regardless, we will be affected by the gossip, the murmuring, the evil reports. And each day we have decisions to make as to whether we will allow these words to pollute our spirits or not. If we walk the road of Absalom, we will not only bring heartache to our relationships but have a powerful negative impact on the generations that follow. Or, if we choose to follow the example of Jonathan, we can live free and be a blessing to those around us. I trust this book has been helpful in increasing your awareness of these defiling situations and how to prevent them from creeping into your speech and listening habits. May God richly bless each one of you in your life's endeavors.

Dr. Michael Sedler received his B.A. in political science in 1977 from the University of California, San Diego, and his master's in social work from Eastern Washington University (Cheney, Washington) in 1981. He earned his D.Min. through Christian Life School of Theology in 1997.

An ordained minister who worked nine years as an associate pastor and fifteen years in the public education system, Michael has also been a social worker, administrator, behavior specialist and teacher. He is presently working full-time ministering in churches and providing consultation services to schools and businesses throughout the United States. He works as an adjunct professor for three universities. Other experiences include work at a state correctional facility for juveniles, as a state trainer in autism and for a community mental health agency.

Michael and his wife, Joyce, have three sons, Jason, Aaron and Luke, as well as a wonderful daughter-in-law and two exceptional grandchildren. Michael grew up in a Jewish home in Phoenix. At the age of 13 he had a bar mitzvah, with confirmation following at the age of 16. Despite these strong Jewish roots, he experienced a spiritual longing in his life that was filled at age 22 when God apprehended him. Michael has called Jesus Christ his Lord and Savior ever since.

Michael and Joyce have developed and presented marriage enrichment seminars for local churches. They taught a nine-month adult discipleship program within their local church for four years. Together they have provided countless hours of individual and marriage counseling and guidance.

Michael is the author of *When to Speak Up and When to Shut Up* and *Stopping Words That Hurt: Positive Words in a World Gone Negative* (both Chosen Books). He has appeared on radio and television programs throughout North America and is frequently asked to provide seminars and training in the areas of communication, motivation, leadership training and marriage principles to churches and businesses.

To contact the author, write to:

Michael Sedler
Sedler Ministries
6505 S. Waneta Rd.
Spokane, WA 99223
509-443-1605
509-443-0111 (fax)
email: michael@michaelsedler.com
website: www.michaelsedler.com

Michael is available for leadership training sessions as well as for other speaking engagements such as in-services, church ministry, conferences or retreats. He is actively involved in training activities throughout the United States and Canada. He has worked extensively with churches, businesses and schools. You will find his approach both practical and informative.

More from Michael D. Sedler

✔Chosen